THE
GALAPAGOS
ISLANDS AND ECUADOR

THE
GALAPAGOS
ISLANDS AND ECUADOR

YOUR ESSENTIAL HANDBOOK FOR EXPLORING DARWIN'S ENCHANTED ISLANDS

MARYLEE STEPHENSON

3RD EDITION

MOUNTAINEERS
BOOKS

Mountaineers Books is the nonprofit publishing division of The Mountaineers, an organization founded in 1906 and dedicated to the exploration, preservation, and enjoyment of outdoor and wilderness areas.

MOUNTAINEERS BOOKS 1001 SW Klickitat Way, Suite 201, Seattle, WA 98134
800.553.4453, www.mountaineersbooks.org

Printed in China
Distributed in the United Kingdom by Cordee, www.cordee.co.uk

First edition, 1989. Second edition, 2000. Third edition, 2015.

Copyeditor: Jane Crosen
Cover and book design: Jen Grable
Cartographer: Marge Mueller, Gray Mouse Graphics

Cover photograph: *Galapagos tortoise* © PeskyMonkey, istockphoto.com
Frontispiece: *Close-up of a blue-footed booby on Seymour Norte* © Alexander Shalamov, istockphoto.com
All photographs by author unless noted otherwise

Library of Congress Cataloging-in-Publication Data
Stephenson, Marylee.
   The Galapagos Islands and Ecuador : your essential handbook for exploring Darwin's enchanted islands / Marylee Stephenson.—3rd edition.
      pages cm
   Enlarged edition of: The Galapagos Islands. 2nd edition, revised and updated. 2005.
   ISBN 978-1-59485-917-5 (pbk.)—ISBN 978-1-59485-918-2 (ebook)
   1. Natural history—Galapagos Islands—Guidebooks. 2. Natural history—Ecuador—Guidebooks. 3. Galapagos Islands—Guidebooks. 4. Ecuador—Guidebooks. I. Stephenson, Marylee. Galapagos Islands. II. Title.
   QH198.G3S73 2015
   508.866'5—dc23
                                        2015004019

ISBN (paperback): 978-1-59485-917-5
ISBN (ebook): 978-1-59485-918-2

To my mother,

Carey Margaret Stephenson,

1914–1995

. . . .

Curiosity is, in great and generous minds,

the first passion and the last.

—*Samuel Johnson,* Rambler, No. 150

Giant tortoise, Santa Cruz

ELEGY FOR THE GIANT TORTOISES

Let others pray for the passenger pigeon
the dodo, the whooping crane, the eskimo:
everyone must specialize

I will confine myself to a meditation
upon the giant tortoises
withering finally on a remote island.

I concentrate in subway stations,
in parks, I can't quite see them,
they move to the peripheries of my eyes

but on the last day they will be there;
already the event
like a wave travelling shapes vision:

on the road where I stand they will materialize,
plodding past me in a straggling line
awkward without water

their small heads pondering
from side to side, their useless armour
sadder than tanks and history,

in their closed gaze ocean and sunlight paralysed,
lumbering up the steps, under the archways
toward the square glass altars

where the brittle gods are kept,
the relics of what we have destroyed,
our holy and obsolete symbols.

From Selected Poems by Margaret Atwood, published by
Houghton Mifflin in 1976. Reprinted with permission.

OVERVIEW MAP OF THE GALAPAGOS ISLANDS

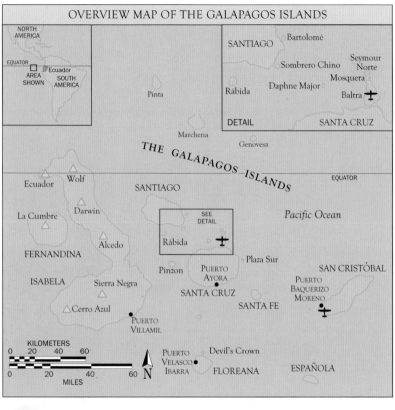

NORTH AMERICA

EQUATOR

AREA SHOWN

Ecuador

SOUTH AMERICA

SANTIAGO

Bartolomé

Sombrero Chino

Seymour Norte

Mosquera

Rábida

Daphne Major

Pinta

Baltra

DETAIL

SANTA CRUZ

Marchena

Genovesa

THE GALAPAGOS ISLANDS

Ecuador

Wolf

SANTIAGO

EQUATOR

La Cumbre

Darwin

SEE DETAIL

Pacific Ocean

Rábida

Alcedo

FERNANDINA

Plaza Sur

SAN CRISTÓBAL

Pinzon

PUERTO AYORA

ISABELA

Sierra Negra

PUERTO BAQUERIZO MORENO

SANTA CRUZ

Cerro Azul

SANTA FE

PUERTO VILLAMIL

KILOMETERS

0 20 40 60

N

PUERTO VELASCO IBARRA

Devil's Crown

FLOREANA

ESPAÑOLA

0 20 40 60

MILES

MAP KEY

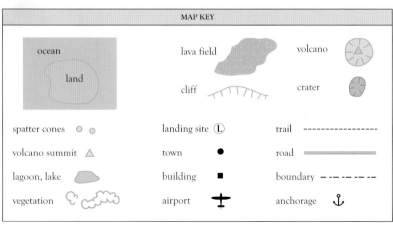

ocean	lava field	volcano
land	cliff	crater
spatter cones	landing site (L)	trail - - - - - -
volcano summit △	town ●	road ===
lagoon, lake	building ■	boundary — - — - — -
vegetation	airport ✈	anchorage ⚓

CONTENTS

Nazca booby and chick, Española

ACKNOWLEDGMENTS

The Galapagos are a very important place for me. Over the last thirty-five years I have made ten visits to the islands, traveling on a variety of boats, with trips lasting up to two weeks. I visited many sites several times and some sites only once. As part of each trip, I visited the highlands of Ecuador and the cloud or rain-forest environments. My Galapagos live-aboard boat travel ranged from tiny, hand-hewn converted fishing craft to motoryachts, motorsailing vessels, and one of the hundred-passenger cruise ships. Each visit has had its own character.

I interviewed staff at both the Galapagos National Park Directorate, and the Charles Darwin Research Station on most of these visits. In preparing for this revision of my guidebook, I also spent another week in Puerto Ayora on Santa Cruz, talking with people actively engaged in research, tourism, and advocacy. From naturalist guides and boat crews, to staff at the Charles Darwin Research Station, Galapagos National Park Directorate, and the Galapagos Conservancy, many people have contributed to my enjoyment of these islands, but in particular I would like to thank Diego Andrade, the guide for my first trip, who continues to be an active guide. He set a very high standard that inspired and informed me from the very beginning.

As I have worked on the revisions to this edition, I have received invaluable advice, comments, suggestions, and corrections from a number of friends and colleagues. I want to emphasize the assistance of Roslyn Cameron, a friend since she worked on the previous edition of this book. Ros has been on staff at the Charles Darwin Foundation for decades, and most recently joined the Galapagos Conservancy. She has reviewed and advised me on the many iterations of this edition, and her patience, humor, and skill are invaluable to me. I must also thank Ros and her artist son, Mason Leon, for their informal hospitality, which added greatly to my latest trips.

I would also like to thank Allie Almario, vice president of Myths and Mountains (www.mythsandmountains.com) and former executive director of the International

Galapagos Tour Operators Association (IGTOA), for her overview of travel to the Galapagos and for reviewing the manuscript as a whole.

Then there is the text treatment, the endless changes, the formatting—usually with tight deadlines. Jeannie McIntosh has always been there for this assistance, for which I am very grateful indeed.

Most of my island trips have been arranged by my friend and travel agent, Jeanneth Vasconez and her partner, Manolo Marin, of Servicios Turisticos Blueline, in Quito. These trips included not only the Galapagos arrangements, but the wonderful itineraries in mainland Ecuador. Of the guides I have traveled with on mainland Ecuador, I would like to thank three in particular not only for their skilled guiding but for their very patient review of this revision of the Ecuador chapters: Patricia Alvarez of Native Ecuador, Giovanna Hermosa, and birder extraordinaire Antonio Torres. I also want to thank Lorena Tapia for a brief but wonderful visit to the historic village of San Miguel de Nono, with her Villa Doris bed-and-breakfast and its hummingbirds.

Over the years, I have traveled to the Galapagos with dear friends and relatives and with small groups of visitors who've come along as part of mini-tours I facilitated. There have been many of them, but I would like to thank especially my first Galapagos travel companion, my dear friend Pamela Sachs. Even if we live a continent apart, we still speak of that marvelous time when the islands were so different, though their enchantment remains. I also want to thank Walter Tschinkel, my biology/science "mentor" since university days, for helping me learn how to learn about the natural world. Thanks also to Mike Weir for his equipment tips for my latest trips.

Finally, my thanks go to editor in chief Kate Rogers, editor Laura Shauger, and designer Jen Grable, all at Mountaineers Books, and to copyeditor Jane Crosen and cartographer Marge Mueller. Naturally, although I received so much help from all the people noted here, any errors in the book are my own.

Opposite: *View from the peak of Bartolomé*

PART I

NATURAL AND CULTURAL HISTORY OF THE GALAPAGOS

1

THE LIVING LABORATORY

What havoc the introduction of any new beast of prey must

cause in a country, before the instincts of the indigenous inhabitants

have become adapted to the stranger's craft or power.

—*Charles Darwin,* The Voyage of the Beagle

For nearly a century and a half, since Charles Darwin's visit in 1835, the Galapagos Islands have been recognized as a living laboratory for the study of biological evolution. Much more recently, it has become clear that these exotic islands provide even more comprehensive lessons—lessons about the very future of life on the planet—with the Galapagos teaching us how easily life can be destroyed and how difficult it is to reverse or even slow that destruction. Yet the Galapagos are also a striking example of how individuals and organizations from around the globe, working with islanders themselves, can cooperate to meet the immense challenges of rapid environmental and social change that face the islands.

A UNIQUE BIOLOGICAL RESOURCE

We are accustomed to thinking of conservation in relation to a biological environment, of its life-forms, land, and water. But of course, conservation must include much more than that, because we are an integral part of the ecosystem and conservation can arise only out of our endeavors. The Galapagos are so fragile, so much the subject of negative external influences, that the day-to-day struggle of those who work on and for these precious islands is both to restore the original life-forms to as near to the state they enjoyed before centuries of human activities on the islands, while at the same time achieving a sustainable human community with a balanced use of natural resources.

The work of restoring the islands, and reversing the negative impacts of human visitation and occupation combined with the impacts of climate change, is moving as rapidly as possible. There are many encouraging stories of successful research, restoration, and community-building activities to which visitors can contribute. Your trip will offer you endless opportunities to learn about the islands. Armed with knowledge and memories, you (along with every visitor) have the opportunity to help increase public awareness, promote international environmental advocacy, or directly support research and restoration in the Galapagos.

The Galapagos Archipelago

The Galapagos are an archipelago, volcanic in origin, located about 1000 kilometers (621 miles) directly west of Ecuador. They straddle the equator, extending 220 kilometers (137 miles) north to south. There are thirteen main islands, seventeen smaller islands, and more than one hundred islets. The islands range in size from Isabela at 500 square kilometers (193 square miles) in area to Plaza Sur, which is only 0.13 square kilometer (0.05 square mile).

The islands are a national park of Ecuador. Almost 97 percent of the landmass, and all of the waters within a 40-mile radius off the archipelago's baseline coast, are preserved and protected as a national park and marine reserve. There are several settlements in the archipelago; the largest are Puerto Ayora on Santa Cruz and Puerto Baquerizo Moreno on San Cristóbal.

The total population of the islands is about 28,000, with more than 200,000 visitors each year. Somewhat more than 30 percent of those who come to the islands are Ecuadoreans, a very important segment of visitors, because this experience can do much to enhance their pride in this province of their home country. They can play a key role in creating and sustaining significant positive changes for the Galapagos. Their support for restoring the islands and their cooperation in preventing the introduction of foreign plants and animals is crucial to the long-range healing and conservation of the Galapagos.

Visitors are very much a part of Galapagos history; while human activities (such as tourism) constitute one of the greatest impacts and threats, they are also the best hope for preserving the islands' quality of life—for humans, plants, and animals. To understand that idea more fully and to fit visitors in their own ecological niche in this marvelous environment, you'll need to look briefly at the natural and human history of the Galapagos.

Endemic Life-Forms of the Galapagos

Far-flung islands are particularly appropriate places to study specific biological processes because their flora and fauna are less diverse than those of the older, larger continental landmasses. Islands of fairly recent volcanic origin, such as the Galapagos, have had less time for soil to develop. If the lack of time is accompanied by extremely high or low rainfall in the area or by extremes of temperature (as would be the case near Earth's poles), then soil development is further retarded. Poor soil means less plant development, and hence fewer life-forms that the land can support.

Just as the problems of and opportunities for survival on far-off islands are distinctive, or even unique, so may be the life-forms that evolve in such isolation. Species that are found only in a specific locale are said to be *endemic*. The Galapagos are famous for their endemic species such as the marine iguana, the only oceangoing iguana in the world. The flightless cormorant is another example. The endemic products of evolution are a constant source of fascination for the visitor, whether tourist or scientist.

The fact that island systems like the Galapagos are distant from a mainland mass means that there are obstacles to

Galapagos penguin on Isabela

Waved albatross, Española

natural transporting of animal or plant life to the islands' shores. The life-forms found on such islands are ones that can withstand the long period of exposure to the sun, wind, and salt water that the accidental journey entails. Life-forms that make a landfall, particularly early in an island's history, may find little or no soil, little or no fresh water, and few other plants or animals to provide sustenance. They may find no others of their own species, which would prevent reproduction (unless fertilization had already taken place). Plants that rely on cross-fertilization for their reproduction face the same problem—what if no other of their species comes their way? Such obstacles to transportation, sustenance, and reproduction can skew the types and proportions of different life-forms found on islands.

On the Galapagos, for instance, the largest endemic plant is *Scalesia pedunculata*, a tree-sized relative of the daisies (*Compositae*). We are used to seeing wild daisies, and their relatives nodding in the breeze in open fields, supported by stems of a few centimeters in diameter and having a height of half a meter at most. But in the Galapagos *Scalesia* "trees" can grow as tall as 20 meters (65 feet), even though they are not true trees with real bark and tree-like circulatory systems.

In the animal world of the Galapagos, the predominant forms are reptiles. Reptiles can endure long periods without food or fresh water and could be transported fairly easily from the South American mainland on the rafts of soil and vegetation carried by river and ocean currents out to sea. The giant tortoise and the land and marine iguanas have come to characterize these islands, lending biological distinctiveness and capturing public interest.

Amphibians and mammals cannot withstand weeks of baking sun and little or no food, so endemic land mammals are few. There are no endemic amphibians on the islands.

The endemic terrestrial mammals are two bat species and several rat species. There were twelve rat species, but four have become extinct because of the overwhelming competition for food and space that resulted from the introduction of black rats (*Rattus rattus*) and Norway rats (*R. norvegicus*). Of the Galapagos mammals, the visitor will be most aware of the marine species: the fur seals, sea lions, and several whale and porpoise species found in these waters.

Birdlife in the Galapagos also reflects the island effect, as do the plant and other animal life-forms. Because birds can fly great distances, many seagoing (pelagic) species are very evident, though few are found only in the Galapagos. Boobies, frigate birds, tropicbirds, pelicans, shearwaters, petrels, and noddy terns are frequently encountered. The same species can be found hundreds or even thousands of miles away in other lands and seas. The waved albatross, although it patrols thousands of square kilometers of ocean for food, is another fascinating example of Galapagos endemism. It easily travels great distances to feed, yet almost all breeding pairs in the world breed on one tiny Galapagos island, Española, with colonies of some ten thousand pairs there.

The other endemic oceangoing bird species are much more limited in range. There are about one thousand penguins, a species unique to the islands, two gull species, and the flightless cormorant. These penguins, gulls, and cormorants do not stray far from their island home. However these birds may have arrived, they have been confined to the area ever since and have evolved into distinct species over great lengths of time.

Proportionately more land-based bird species, such as the Darwin's finches, are endemic to the islands. Reasons for this are complex, but the situation is linked to the great distances between the islands and the mainland—limiting the numbers

Guide explaining the active volcanoes of Isabela

of arrivals in the first place, and then making it more likely that they will evolve independently in separate island homes.

Advantages and Vulnerability of Far-Flung Environments

Despite the difficulties of reaching the islands and the problems of reproduction, there is a potential advantage. Those who do survive may find little competition from other organisms. A plant that had to struggle elsewhere for enough nutrients, light, and space may find a surfeit of each on a distant island not colonized by other plants, or at least not by plants with very similar needs for survival.

A bird that formerly had to fly long distances over water and then dive ceaselessly just to get enough food may find rich pickings right next to the shore. A finchlike bird that fed on a few kinds of seeds may learn how to feed on insects, although in its place of origin that food was taken by woodpeckers. An animal that was preyed upon by carnivores may find itself in a location where these predators do not exist. And over hundreds of thousands of years, the newcomer may lose its genetically based wariness of the unfamiliar.

The processes of evolution, the mechanisms of natural selection, are too complex to elaborate upon here. But very distant islands such as the Galapagos are prime locations for learning about evolutionary processes. A visit to the islands can give a sense of immediacy, of a connection with these processes that no text, picture book, or movie can equal.

Gigantism is common in these circumstances, and the islands support huge land tortoises, giant *Scalesia*, and ferns the size of trees. Flightlessness is common; the Galapagos Islands have a flightless cormorant. Also common is a proliferation of closely related species filling distinct ecological niches only a few meters in altitude or a valley or mountaintop away. The fourteen well-known species of Darwin's finches, believed to have come from a common finchlike ancestor and now each distinct in its habits and appearance, are examples of this process. Some species are found in only a few places, others in many, and some overlap in their range. The four mockingbird species endemic to the archipelago tell a similar story. And the fearlessness of the animals in the Galapagos in the face of introduced threats, such as humans, also is characteristic of animal life on isolated islands.

The formation of new and different plant and animal species is called *adaptive radiation*. Species adapt to fill new or previously available niches in a new way. Visitors to the islands see examples of this process at every turn. The guides are trained to point out the distinct characteristics of the plants and animals and to identify those that are endemic or indigenous. Introduced plant and animal species are evident, as is their generally negative impact. The behavioral distinctiveness also is very clear; the animals' calm acceptance of human visitors makes a trip to the Galapagos a truly impressive and moving experience.

But these same qualities of far-flung islands can be the source of their extreme vulnerability. Shallow soil can be swept away in moments during torrential rain if the trees that anchored it have been razed for grazing by domestic animals. Fearless animals can be killed by the outstretched hand. Darwin speaks of birds so unsuspecting that they could be struck down with a stick. Predatory animals that are introduced suddenly to the island can devour eggs laid in sand or burrows. If the threat is strong enough, whether that is from an animal, another plant, a virus, or bacteria, it is likely the original organism will be extinguished. There will not be enough time, or the necessary conditions, to adapt to this new threat.

Giant tortoise snacking on a cactus

Today's visitor has come just in time to the Galapagos—in time to see the effects of human interference on biological processes and to see just how quickly habitat can change and species be lost. Yet this is also the right time to see how humans are working to arrest and even reverse that destruction, as you will learn during your visit there.

HUMAN HISTORY

The written record of the human history of the Galapagos begins with records of Fray Tomás de Berlanga, who in 1535 was Bishop of Panama and the highest representative of the Catholic Church in the Spanish territories of the Americas. Fray Tomás was sent on a troubleshooting mission to Peru, under orders from Holy Roman Emperor Charles V. Tomás's ship, becalmed off the west coast of South America, drifted to what we now know as the Galapagos. Fray Tomás sent men ashore on several islands to look for desperately needed water. His description (quoted in J. R. Slevin's history *The*

Galapagos Islands) of what they saw and did has a familiar ring, echoed in the diaries of pirates and mapmakers and whalers over the centuries.

They found nothing but seals, and turtles, and such big tortoises that each could carry a man on top of itself and many iguanas that are like serpents. [On another island] the same conditions prevailed as on the first; many seals, turtles, iguanas, tortoises, many birds like those of Spain, but so silly that they do not know how to flee, and many were caught in the hand.

Much of the human history that followed is similar. People landed to search for water and rarely found it. They saw a place that was bizarre and inhospitable. They noticed the fearlessness of the animals and took full advantage of it for "sport" and for food, which meant mostly tortoise meat. It was the Spanish word for "tortoise," *galápago*, that eventually stuck as the name for the islands. It replaced the earlier name, Encantadas, Spanish for "enchanted" or "bewitched." (This name apparently arose out of the baffling, treacherous currents around the islands or the peculiar light conditions and mist and fogs that made the islands appear and disappear from a distance, in a miragelike fashion.)

Early explorers were followed by (or overlapped with) buccaneers. South America and its wealth, both real and imagined, were hotly contested by the French,

Spanish, and English. Naturally, the waters around it were the scene of many struggles for power and booty. The Galapagos provided a hideout for buccaneers, offering them sporadic water supplies and regular supplies of tortoise meat. This use of the islands by pirates continued through much of the eighteenth century.

The nineteenth century saw the islands exposed to the largest and most destructive wave of human visitation: the whalers. The buccaneers slaughtered animals, and they probably introduced rats, cats, and other highly destructive animals. But for sheer numbers, no other groups were as large as the aggregate numbers of whaling ships and their crews. In one estimate, based on whaling ship records, at least seven hundred whaling ships plied the Pacific between 1811 and 1844. Any one ship that came to the islands took up to six hundred tortoises on board. (Another estimate of the rate of depletion: in one thirty-year period, more than two hundred thousand tortoises were taken from the islands.)

Sought after because they provided fresh meat for the long voyages, tortoises were stacked in the holds and could live as long as a year without food or water. Considering the atrocious quality of food on most sea voyages of the time, the appeal of fresh meat is obvious.

The numbers of tortoises that originally existed on the islands must have been phenomenal to have withstood this kind of destruction for at least two centuries. But by 1846, there were no tortoises left on Floreana, and those on Rábida and Santa Fe became extinct around that time as well.

The only thing that saved the few remaining tortoises was that the same rapacity shown to them was applied to whales. In the mid-1800s whale stocks became so low that the whaling industry virtually collapsed. Whalers' visits to the Galapagos ended by 1865.

Enter Charles Darwin

Of course, the explorers, buccaneers, and whalers brought with them the maritime arm of authority. Naval ships from various countries occasionally visited the islands, sometimes by accident, sometimes as part of explorations for mapping or finding dependable locations for water or food.

It was as a part of the English Admiralty's worldwide mapping efforts that Charles Darwin came to the Galapagos for five weeks in 1835. As the naturalist on the *Beagle*, he visited several of the islands. He recounts in some detail the varied characteristics of the wildlife, including the notable fearlessness. His account of his visit in *The Voyage of the Beagle* is very readable and highly recommended.

On a visit to the Floreana Island home of the archipelago's acting governor, Darwin was told that it was possible to tell which island a tortoise came from by noting the differences in the shape of its shell, or carapace. This circumstance and the unique forms of birdlife were seminal in Darwin's thoughts on the role of natural selection in evolution.

If you have a chance to read the Galapagos section of Darwin's book before your trip, bring photocopies of those pages. You can read his account and travel in his footsteps here and there. Your path won't necessarily be the same, but you will see parts of the same islands and many of the same plants and animals as he did.

By the time Darwin arrived on the islands, there had already been some human settlement. In 1832, an attempt was made to colonize the islands with reprieved mutineers from the Ecuadorean army. (Because their choice was to serve as colonists or be executed, their enthusiasm for the project can well be imagined.) Shortly thereafter, another penal colony was established on Floreana. The cruelty of the colony's overseers became notorious throughout the century that it continued to exist.

The nineteenth century saw several more attempts to colonize the islands to extract lichens, salt, or sulfur or to grow crops such as sugar cane. None succeeded, and when the end came to most of these projects, it was a violent one.

Unanticipated, Unwelcome Visitors

Buccaneers, whalers, and colonizers didn't simply take from the islands; they gave—not out of a spirit of charity but rather the willing or accidental introduction of a wide variety of foreign plants and animals. These early visitors came and went, but the goats, cats, rats, fire ants, and guava plants—all gone wild and taking over the space and food sources of endemic species—are still in evidence. A more recent introduction, known locally as the "blackberry" (but in reality, the hill raspberry bush, *Rubus niveus*), is another challenge for endemic species. So the struggle against the introduction of harmful plants and animals continues, as these are transported through a wide variety of modern human activities.

Toward the end of the 1800s, scientific interest in the islands increased, and there were periodic expeditions to the archipelago. Their goals may have been benign (although we may question the collector mentality these days), but their impact on the fragile Galapagos ecosystem was not. While some were for scientific purposes, others were to fill niches in the collections of a particular expedition's wealthy sponsors. Whatever the purpose, specimens were collected in large numbers, often with little or no scientific justification, while the locals readily supplied the collectors and crews with food from rapidly dwindling wildlife resources.

The vivid accounts of some of the scientists who visited the islands in the early twentieth century led some people, particularly in Norway, to believe that the Galapagos could be developed as a utopia. Several individuals and families tried to make a go of it, but very few succeeded. Detailed accounts of these attempts have been published. Descendants of a few of these European families still live on the

ISLAND NAMES

Because the Galapagos archipelago has a long, complicated history of "ownership" or sovereignty, the individual islands have as many as four names, in at least two languages. For scientists and tour companies and visitors using their home languages, the nomenclature may well be in their first language and in neither Spanish nor English. However, because the trend now in the Galapagos, for research and tourism purposes, is to use the Spanish names, I have followed that style throughout this book, with only a couple of exceptions where the English language name is in such general use that it would be confusing to use the Spanish.

islands. A small number of Ecuadorean nationals also came at this time, because the land was free to whoever was willing to try farming in the difficult environment. Their descendants are active in many of the islands' contemporary social and economic aspects.

The islands deteriorated rapidly in the next several decades as a slowly increasing population did all it could to shape the natural environment into one suitable for farming, ranching, and village living. Trees were cut to clear grazing land. Open areas were burned for agricultural reasons, then overtaken by plants that had been introduced as potential crops and had spread beyond the farmers' fencing.

The new plants often succeeded too well; sometimes the land wasn't even useful for pasture because they formed dense thickets inhospitable for domestic animals. Where ground cover was lost, erosion of sloping land was widespread. It doesn't rain often in the Galapagos, but when it does, during the annual torrential rains and even more so during extreme events such as El Niño, it rains in torrents that erode unprotected soil.

Wildlife, including tortoises, was hunted. Burros and goats ate up valuable plant food and trampled ground nesting sites. The predations of many vulnerable native animals by introduced mammals, such as cats, dogs, and rats, continued unabated.

The human history of the islands, as portrayed in the superb exhibits of the Interpretive Center in Puerto Baquerizo Moreno, on San Cristóbal, is a fascinating and often distressing trip through the last five hundred years. You will also learn about change and hope for the future.

SAYING NO TO DESTRUCTION

Although much of the early scientific work in the Galapagos was detrimental to the island wildlife, scientists' activities have led to positive changes. Beginning in the 1930s, as the global and Ecuadorean political will to protect the islands began to strengthen and resources for conservation began to be allocated, positive changes started to gather momentum. The 1935 Galapagos Memorial Expedition, composed of an international team of scientists visiting the islands to commemorate the hundredth anniversary of Darwin's visit, focused the attention of the international scientific community on these fragile islands. The Ecuadorean government passed legislation aimed at protecting island wildlife, but it had little enforcement capacity, and World War II interrupted this progress.

In 1959, another landmark for the renewal of the islands was the hundredth anniversary of the publication of Darwin's *The Origin of Species*. That year, the combined efforts of Ecuadorean conservationists and international scientific and conservation groups resulted in the establishment of the two basic building blocks of the renewed Galapagos: the Ecuadorean government's declaration that all of the

Colorful marine iguana, Española

viduals. The Charles Darwin Foundation continues to carry out important research at its operative arm, the Charles Darwin Research Station (CDRS), in Puerto Ayora, on Santa Cruz Island. In the 1960s, efforts to create understanding and cooperation among the then two thousand local inhabitants around the Research Station and its important conservation projects were largely successful, boding well for the long-term prospects.

Species and Habitat Restoration Projects

After the station's construction was completed in 1964, researchers began island projects. They launched the tortoise captive breeding program in 1965 with eggs brought from Pinzon Island, and the first of the iconic Española adult tortoises were soon added. The first steps were taken to control the feral animals, including eliminating the goats on little Plaza Sur Island.

Three years later, the Galapagos National Park Directorate (Park Service) was set up under the direct guidance of the Ecuadorean government. The first park superintendent started work in 1972. Over the years, with a substantial increase in its resources, including more wardens and patrol boats, the Park Service has grown to become the authority responsible for the management of the protected areas.

The Galapagos National Park Directorate, with the help of partners such as

islands (exclusive of already-settled areas) were to become a national park, protected from all forms of destructive use, and the establishment of the Charles Darwin Foundation. The foundation was supported by the World Conservation Union (now the International Union for Conservation of Nature, or IUCN) and UNESCO, as well as other groups and indi-

the Charles Darwin Foundation, continues to develop programs for predator control, captive breeding of vulnerable animals, the return of these threatened species to their home islands (when it is safe to do so), and habitat restoration. One example is the 2011 study of the interactions among giant tortoises, albatross, woody vegetation, and cactus on Española Island. This multifaceted research is designed to identify the management actions necessary to restore habitat for both giant tortoises and the albatross. Captive rearing of tortoises is only part of the solution if they have no food on their home island. Complex, complementary research will ensure that scientists' responses for protecting and sustaining the ecosystem as a whole are appropriate and holistic.

The collaboration of the Park Service and Research Station has made it possible to include the station's expertise in scientific and conservation matters as an integral part of training that all Park Service guides must undertake before they are licensed to work on boats. The station also takes part in the courses given to regularly update guides on the latest research findings and other news about the islands. The guides bring tourists their enhanced scientific knowledge and also make sure that they follow the simple but important park rules: don't disturb the animals, don't pick the flowers, and clean your shoes carefully when leaving any site and boarding the boat (so that seeds from one island are not

introduced to another). This crucial training ensures that visitors treat the islands with enlightened respect and come away with a genuine understanding of their global and local value.

The guides also help call attention to any changes to visitor sites. They are out every day in nearly every corner of the archipelago, and they notice sudden changes, such as volcanic eruptions, unusual mortality of Galapagos animals, or any changes in the presence and impacts of introduced animals. In 2014, for instance, guides reported two rare bird sightings in one week—a first sighting of a juvenile penguin at the far northern island of Genovesa and a vermilion flycatcher (*Pyrocephalus rubinus*) on Rábida. The last sighting of this beautiful bird there was recorded in 1906!

Predator Control

Control, much less total eradication, of feral dogs, goats, burros, cats, and rats is extraordinarily difficult, though the decades of dedicated effort are paying off. Goats were eliminated from Santiago by 2009—more than one hundred thousand over a thirty-year effort! In 2011–14 a major rat eradication project was undertaken on Rábida Island, following successful work on Seymour Norte.

Rat eradication on Pinzon Island was successful in 2012 after nearly fifty years of trying various means to extirpate them. The island is continuously monitored, and as of 2014, it appears to be a

Sea turtle tracks, Floreana

success. Indeed, a survey of tortoises in 2014 revealed a number of very young ones doing well. It is estimated that three hundred to five hundred tortoises are now thriving on their own there. Rat eradication is being planned for Floreana Island, building on lessons learned from the earlier experiences.

Feral dogs, cats, and burros are no longer the considerable threat they have been, because they have been controlled or eliminated from many key areas. In 2005 feral cats were eradicated from Baltra, the island where many visitors first arrive. You may see land iguanas as you go to your bus to meet your boat, or waiting for the ferry to Puerto Ayora, because they are now reproducing successfully and can often be seen near the airport.

The struggle to eradicate pigs was successful on Santiago Island in 2001. In 2006 feral goats were eradicated on northern Isabela and Santiago islands, using an intensive hunting program, with the aid of trained hunting dogs and aerial hunting from helicopters. Eradicating goats on northern Isabela, one of the major islands of the archipelago, has been of inestimable value for the survival and increase of giant tortoises, sea turtles, and Galapagos petrels and rails (both ground-nesting birds). This achievement was made possible through the support of the Global Environmental Facility, with vital counterpart funding from the travelers with Lindblad Expeditions and the members of Galapagos Conservancy, many of whom have become active in helping after a visit. This support from the tourism sector has been the key to this success story and many others.

One of the most heartening stories of successful restoration has been with the giant tortoises of Española (Hood) Island. Although there were no introduced predators on this arid island, the endemic tortoise population almost disappeared when their food source, the naturally scanty vegetation, was further reduced by large herds of goats introduced decades before. The surviving tortoises became so few and so scattered that males and females never met; through the first half of the twentieth century there was no evidence of any Española tortoises breeding. In the 1960s, only fourteen of these animals were located there, all brought in for captive rearing. By 2014, more than one thousand captive-reared individuals have been returned to Española.

Despite all the difficulties, the slide of tortoise and land iguana populations into extinction has indeed slowed, although control sometimes still depends on taking the few remaining individuals to the two Park Service's tortoise breeding centers (on Santa Cruz and San Cristóbal) for rearing. Once they reproduce, and the young are three to five years old, they usually can be returned to their home island, or in some cases placed on an island on which they once existed. While tortoises and iguanas are being "rescued" and repatriated to the natural environment, they are still *vulnerable* or *endangered* because their continued existence relies so heavily on interventions by scientists, park staff, and the many local, national, and international supporters.

Amphibians have arrived by hitch-hiking on the increasingly numerous cargo ships supplying the growing tourism industry and resident population from the mainland. During the wet years of the 1997–98 El Niño, small tree-dwelling frogs of the species *Scinax quinquefasciata* arrived from the coastal lowlands of Ecuador so often and in such numbers (hitch-hiking in cargo) that they could establish and survive. Despite control efforts, this species has spread to inhabited areas where humans tend to accumulate water for household use or gardening or farming. These arrivals breed at very rapid rates, eating insects and spiders and thereby reducing this food supply for the birds and other endemic species that rely on this resource.

Introduced species, whether plant or animal, require costly and often creative solutions. It often takes massive efforts to clean up the actions of one thoughtless individual. Early identification of these invaders and substantial investment in eradication is the result of decades of outreach to residents. For example, in 2009 the introduction of the giant African land snail required extensive sterilization of entire farms by authorities. Trained sniffer dogs help identify the snails' presence so that eradicators can decide where to invest their efforts.

The giant African snails threaten the endemic snail fauna in a way that habitat loss has not. The Galapagos *Bulimid* snails are the best example of adaptive radiation on the islands, with nearly ninety species identified from the ancestral source and still counting. But the African snail is known throughout the Pacific and Caribbean for its ability to destroy local snail populations, and so the response to eradicate them has been very rapid indeed.

Success Milestones

However, with all the frustrations of restoration work, the overall story is one of success—success with the many projects being established and the arduous steps that can begin to reverse and even halt the ravages of the past and protect against the threats of the future.

Two major milestones in the Galapagos story occurred twenty years apart. The first was in 1978, when the Galapagos National Park was named a World Heritage Site by UNESCO. The enormous economic and prestige value of receiving such a designation and being a significant international tourism destination encourages the local communities and the Ecuadorean government in their efforts to renew and maintain this precious resource.

The second milestone was in 1998, with the creation of the Special Law for Galapagos. This law redefined the area of the Galapagos Marine Reserve, enlarging it to about 64 kilometers (40 miles) out from the coast of all the islands. The Galapagos National Park Directorate administers this reserve as well as all the protected land areas, and counts on technical support from the Charles Darwin Foundation and many other national and international partners as well as local stakeholders. The Special Law is complex, and its provisions include the restriction of fishing except for artisanal (nonindustrial) methods by local resident fishers and the creation of a quarantine program.

This program includes a predeparture inspection before people and cargo leave mainland Ecuador, inspecting and fumigating arriving vessels and planes coming to the islands, checking luggage for plant or animal products that are prohibited, and also inspecting the luggage and cargo being transported from island-to-island. (This is a part of the "island-hopping" process for those who visit on their own, taking speedy boats to other islands to visit the communities there.) Given the variety of means of coming to the islands and of moving among them, preventing the arrival of both marine and land-based invasive species and developing ways of counteracting their impacts when they cannot be evaded is a continuous, vital task for all. Tourists have the opportunity and responsibility to play a positive role in this work.

All of this complex and often colorful history leads us back to visitors and the ecological niche they occupy. The sheer scientific value of the islands alone justifies preserving and managing them with the present approach. But the islands are much more than a living laboratory for the study of evolution; they are also now a pivotal site for learning about how climate change is affecting this special place. Galapagos is also a role model for the world on creating a sustainable use of natural resources and model society living in harmony with the environment that they benefit from. Above all, Galapagos is a place of beauty, to be cherished as an opportunity to have a personal, close, intense experience of a very distinctive natural world.

This is not to say that every islander and every environmentalist or visitor is completely satisfied with the way the islands are governed or controlled. But Galapagos is still a model of worldwide conservation efforts, a model that islanders, scientists, and visitors are supporting by our presence, appreciation, learning, and contributions of time and money. If we all were not involved, there would be little left but a few dry rocks with a lot of rats and goats eating themselves into oblivion.

2

GEOLOGY AND PLANT LIFE

Due to the volcanic processes that have shaped the Galapagos Islands over time (several million years), their topography ranges from steep mountain slopes to coastal lowlands just above sea level. The diverse topography, moisture, and soil conditions result in a range of ecological zones, contributing to the islands' biodiversity.

VOLCANIC PROCESSES

The whole Galapagos archipelago is spread across an area of about 138,000 square kilometers (53,282 square miles), including the landmass and surrounding waters of the Marine Reserve. Galapagos is among the most active volcanic areas in the world, and its volcanic processes are of great scientific importance. The landmass of the islands has resulted from volcanic action that built up the land in one of two ways: layering or uplift.

Most of the islands have the classic conical shape that we associate with volcanic action. Some islands have one dominant cone with small subsidiary cones littering its slopes. (Isabela, for example, has six major volcanic mountains, several of which are active.) These mountainous islands are formed through successive eruptions that build up layer upon layer of lava and ash. This *layering* can happen on existing land or underwater. If it is the latter, the mountain may eventually reach such a size that its peak reaches the surface, forming an island.

By contrast, a few islands, such as Plaza Sur, Baltra, and Seymour Norte, were once flat ocean bottom, but were raised to the surface by shifts of molten material below. This process is called *uplift*, and it gives these islands their characteristic "tilted table" look.

The oldest of the Galapagos islands are on the southeastern edge of the archipelago. Española is more than three million years old. The western islands of Fernandina and Isabela, on the other hand, are less than seven hundred thousand years old.

These islands on the western side of the Galapagos have shown the most recent volcanic activity. There was an eruption of the Fernandina volcano in 1958, obliterating the lake at the bottom of the crater (it reformed two years later). Then in 1968, the crater floor of Fernandina's volcano suddenly sank another 300 meters (1000 feet) below its previous level of 800 meters (2600 feet) below the edge of the rim. (The crater itself is 4 by 6.5 kilometers, about 2.5 by 4 miles, across.) The day the floor was subsiding, more than two hundred earthquakes took place on the island. In 1977 fresh lava poured into its crater, and then in 1978 it had eruptive activity again. It erupted yet again in 1988, 1991, 1995, 2005, and 2009.

Isabela also has a very active recent history of volcanic events. In February 1979 its southernmost volcano, Cerro Azul, erupted over three weeks. Lava was spewed as high as 200 meters (650 feet) into the air. The lava flows reached 10 kilometers (6 miles) in length. It erupted again over two months, starting in September 1998. The Sierra Negra volcano erupted most recently in October 2005. Isabela's Wolf volcano, at the island's northern tip, erupted in 2015, but early reports indicated that there was no significant damage to plant or animal life.

Because of the islands' geological history, their topography is one of many moderately steep slopes, often leading to a major mountain. The height of the islands ranges from just a few meters above sea level (in the case of those that were uplifted or are simply very small) to Wolf volcano, which rises 1707 meters (5600 feet) above sea level. Most visitors stick to the low edges of the islands, but some may have time for a trip to the highlands of Santa Cruz or San Cristóbal. A few may even climb Alcedo volcano, on Isabela.

The range of altitudes has great implications for the amounts of precipitation available at greater heights and for soil development and plant and animal life.

PLANTS AND ECOLOGICAL ZONES

Plant life is the basis of all life in the Galapagos, although it is often overshadowed for the visitor by the animals found there. Yet the plants often are beautiful, and they are surely as interesting. They can tell us about evolutionary processes, and it is important to preserve them against destructive intruders such as other plants, grazing and rooting animals, and people.

The Galapagos are among the best-studied tropical island ecosystems in the world. For more than fifty-five years, since the foundation of the Charles Darwin Research Station, scientists have consistently studied Galapagos biodiversity. Nevertheless, the Charles Darwin Foundation's Galapagos Species Checklist does show that work remains to be done for there to be a complete inventory of the array of species of plant and animal life on the islands. As for plants specifically,

Opuntia *cactus, a spiny beauty*

it appears that there are about fourteen hundred vascular plant species (endemic, native, and introduced, including cultivated species), though there are new identifications regularly. Around six hundred of these species are endemic to the islands. Among the nonvascular plants (such as lichens) there are many newcomers, with first full record of these being documented by the Research Station in recent years. Lichens alone number around six hundred, with some additions new to science.

It is a distressing testimony to the impact of humans over the centuries that introduced plants now outnumber the native plants on the islands, often with very negative results for the native plants. The most aggressive of these introduced species, which have supplanted tens of thousands of acres of native plants, include guava, passionflower, elephant grass, lantana, quinine, and "blackberry." A number of native Galapagos plants are in danger of becoming extinct on the islands and, in the case of endemic species, their extinction is thus worldwide and forever.

The Park Service is actively trying to control or eradicate these threats to island plant life. It is a staggering task, especially with limited budgets. Progress is certainly being made, but so much more remains to be done before success can be achieved. In general terms, the plant life of the Galapagos can be grouped according to ecological zones that roughly follow the altitude profiles and patterns of wind exposure of the islands. These zones are not clearly defined, not only because of the very diverse topography, but because human intervention—agriculture, invasive plants—has changed the original patterns of plant life. There are also differences in the plant literature about the number of ecological zones, but the following divisions should still be useful for visitors observing the general distribution of plants.

Coastal Zone

The lowest zone is the coastal one, and it can be further divided into wet and dry areas. The wet areas are the mangrove thickets that edge low-lying lagoons and shorelines of many of the islands. The dry areas are comprised of beaches and dunes.

The mangrove tree has many strategies for surviving in a very harsh environment. The trees are awash with salty water, and alternately exposed to wet and dry conditions. The mud in which they anchor themselves is extremely oxygen poor. As a means of resisting the salt, the trees are able to retain fresh water from rains, take oxygen directly from the air, and spread their roots very wide in the mud below rather than going down deep into unstable, low-nutrient earth.

Mangroves are like watery forests in that they provide a sheltered home for a rich array of wildlife. Shrimp, crabs, crustaceans, and small fish find shelter there, and in turn provide food for larger fish and for the herons, noddy terns, and pelicans that lurk above waiting for a snack. Sea turtles and several kinds of rays can frequently be seen in the open tidal waters of the mangrove thickets as well.

The dry area of the coastal zone includes the upper beaches, especially the dune areas that are usually above high-tide levels and can support terrestrial plant life. Plant life here consists of low, spreading plants that are very good at retaining moisture and clinging to what little stable sand or soil is available. The most striking is the herb *Sesuvium portulacastrum*, which has stems that turn a brilliant red toward the end of the dry season (roughly October to December). Seeing those mats of color on a gleaming white dune is a memorable experience. You can't miss it on Plaza Sur or on the path at Sombrero Chino.

Arid Lowlands Zone

The arid lowlands zone stretches inland from an island's beaches up to about 60 meters (200 feet) in elevation. It is best envisioned as a desert, for except in the very moist years when the El Niño current sweeps alongside the islands, it is indeed a very dry environment. Here plants are scrubby, thorny, and sparsely spaced. They too have their strategies for retaining moisture and clinging to sandy soil.

This zone is host to some of the more striking cactus plants of the islands: the candelabra cactus (*Jasminocereus thouarsii*), the treelike prickly pear (*Opuntia echios*), and the low-lying prickly pear (*Opuntia helleri*). On recent lava flows such as the one at Sulivan Bay, patches of the short bottle-brush-shaped tubes of the lava cactus (*Brachycereus nesioticus*) are scattered here and there.

In this dry area, it is possible to see vines such as the endemic lava morning glory (*Ipomoea habeliana*) and the endemic passionflower (*Passiflora foetida*). The edible fruit of the introduced species of this latter plant is causing a great deal of

concern because its seeds are easily spread and the aggressive vines smother and outcompete native plants.

As the land slopes upward, the most evident plant is the palo santo tree (*Bursera graveolens*). It is silvery gray, and other than having a rich collection of lichen on its surface, it looks quite dead. There are no leaves much of the time, but when the rare rainy period does come, the leaves burst out, and for a few weeks it has small white flowers. Many of the paths for visitors lead through swaths of these intriguing trees. The palo santo tree has cultural significance, as it is named the "holy tree," because it is a metaphor for the death and resurrection of Jesus. When it is burned it also gives off a pleasant scent, reminiscent

Brachycereus *cactus, early colonizer of lava flows, Fernandina*

of incense used in the Mass ceremony of the Catholic church.

Transition Zone

As the zone name implies, the transition zone has plants characteristic of both the lower arid zone and the somewhat more humid levels above. In general, the vegetation is more dense and less desertlike in its appearance. There are also more plant species than in the arid zone.

In the category of large shrubs or smaller trees there are two common species. One is the pega pega (*Pisonia floribunda*), which is endemic to the islands. Another endemic species is the guayabillo (*Psidium galapageium*), which occurs in this zone and also farther up in the *Scalesia* zone (see below). It has white flowers and a small fruit like the guava (*Psidium guajava*), to which it is related.

Less obvious but equally interesting herbaceous plants of the transition zone are the maidenhair fern (*Adiantum concinnum*) and the Galapagos tomato (*Lycopersicon cheesmanii*), which is endemic to the islands. The latter is salt tolerant. Its fruit is yellow to light orange, contrasting with the very red tomato that was introduced for commercial use and which has hybridized with the endemic species.

Scalesia Zone

This is the first of what are also known as humid zones, although it is named after the treelike plant that characterizes the levels between 300 and 600 meters

(1000 and 2000 feet)—*Scalesia pedunculata*, a member of the order *Compositae*. The *Scalesias* may have been established long ago in the Galapagos because the seeds of the composite family are very light and can be blown for great distances. As the most successful naturally arriving competitor for the soil on the moist upper slopes of the larger islands, these plants achieve considerable height, growing from 5 to 20 meters (16 to 65 feet) tall.

If you are familiar with the towering canopy of tropical rain forests, or the massive cedars and firs of North American temperate rain forests, you may at first not find the *Scalesia* forest to be as impressive. The trees are not as tall, but these forests have a spirit and interest all their own. The trees are draped with great beards of moss and coats of lichen on the branches and trunks. There is a sense of stillness, of being surrounded by a rich, dense world that is a home for many kinds of life.

On inhabited islands, these *Scalesia* forests have been seriously reduced in numbers and range by human-related activities. Land was cleared for planting or grazing. Pigs and goats would root out the seedlings and feed on growing and older plants.

The eradication of goats in some islands in the archipelago has allowed the *Scalesia* to begin to rebound in specific locations, but total recovery is very far away. Plants such as the guava and blackberry have infiltrated nearly all the

Galapagos cotton, Miconia *zone, Santa Cruz*

highlands of the islands; their dense growth pattern squeezes out most other plants in an area. Blackberry and guava are nearly unstoppable once introduced and require constant treatment with site- and plant-specific application of herbicides to the trunks and the grueling work of removal by hand.

As these and other invasive species are difficult and costly to control or eradicate, innovative farmers are companion-planting commercial crops such as coffee and cacao with *Scalesia* to build a new market-directed agricultural industry, while at the same time responding to the need to save native plants. These reinvigorated efforts to expand the productivity and range of Galapagos-sourced commercial products, are demonstrated by the increasing number of greenhouses on the main inhabited islands. These improved agricultural practices also help reduce the need to import many of the basic vegetables and fruits from the mainland, thereby strengthening the local economy.

The importation of plant foods is a major source of introduced, invasive plant species and the principal reason for having the quarantine program, with inspections of cargo and personal baggage, not only for those arriving in the islands but for those who are island-hopping. You will also find that the guides ensure that visitors clean their shoes when reentering the boat after a trail walk, to avoid the transfer of any kind of species from island to island.

Miconia Zone

This zone is named after what was once the dominant plant of this level, Miconia robinsoniana, a shrub that grows 3 to 4 meters high (10 to 13 feet). This zone is the humid level of land just above the Scalesia zone, at about 600 to 700 meters (2000 to 2300 feet). The plant is very attractive, having regular pointed leaves, with very evident grids of veins forming patterns on the shiny leaves. The leaves are shaded at their edges with yellow or red, which adds to their appeal. The Miconia is endemic to the Galapagos and is considered one of the most endangered plants in the islands. Clearing land for cattle grazing has been responsible for much of its destruction on San Cristóbal and Santa Cruz, along with the damage caused by the invasion of the area by aggressive plants like quinine and blackberry.

You are most likely to go to a Miconia area on Santa Cruz. It is a lovely experience, because much progress has been made there in the removal of invasive plants, an essential element in the recovery of the Miconia. This is a tribute to the work of the Park Service wardens in particular. They regularly go to the area and hand-chop and poison the invasive quinine trees—one at a time.

Once you are in the Miconia zone, look on the ground for some of the mosses that grow there. There is a very handsome club moss called Lycopodium clavatum. It grows only about 15 centimeters (6 inches) high, but its prickly green stems make it stand out from the surrounding vegetation beneath your feet. The Galapagos cotton (Gossypium darwinii), endemic to the islands, can be seen here. This humid zone is an important nesting site for the critically endangered Galapagos petrel (Pterodroma phaeopygia), a ground-nesting bird.

Fern and Sedge Zone

The fern and sedge zone (also called the pampa zone) occurs at more than 600 meters (2000 feet). Overall it is the wettest zone of the archipelago. Not all islands have this elevation, so some lack this characteristic vegetation. Also, the amount of rainfall determines whether the plant life in a given high-elevation location is of this type. Some slopes, protected by a mountain from the prevailing moisture-laden winds, may be too dry to have a fern and sedge zone.

These moist and high conditions are very hospitable to sedges, grasses, and ferns. Various mosses and liverworts thrive here as well. No true trees, and few shrubs, grow here. The dominant plant, in the undisturbed state, is the endemic Galapagos tree fern (*Cyathea weatherbyana*). It is quite a shock to see that they are as tall as an adult and that they have fiddleheads as big as a fist.

3

ANIMAL LIFE

My interest in birds brought me to the Galapagos—as my birding knowledge deepened and I read more widely about evolution and adaptation, my interests expanded well beyond my avian dreams. I felt compelled to visit the place that sparked the most important theories of how life begins, changes, and ends in our world. There is much beyond the land birds and seabirds—to see, learn, experience, share, and treasure.

There are the mammals—some invasive, many destructive—and the constant fights to remove them, repair the damage they have caused, and find a sustainable way forward. The reptiles come next—perhaps the most well-known of all the animal life of the islands—iguanas on land and sea, gigantic tortoises on land, beautiful marine turtles slipping below the surface as you quietly paddle in a lagoon. The large reptiles may be the most dramatic, but the lava lizards blink at you from rocks and walls wherever you

may be. And finally, this chapter considers the newest addition to the Galapagos National Park—the Marine Reserve that extends 64 kilometers (40 miles) outside of every point of land in the islands. It both protects and preserves the precious marine environment that shapes the land—and vice versa—and it provides the visitor a new way of communing with this magical place.

BIRDS

You don't have to be a bird-watcher to find birdlife an endless source of enjoyment. And if you are a bird-watcher, you will find yourself in paradise. It isn't so much that there is a large number of species in the islands, rather the appeal is that so many are very distinctive and are endemic, found only there. There are some 178 bird species recorded in the Galapagos, but their status varies. There are forty-four endemic species and subspecies, twelve indigenous species (they breed and live there, but also do elsewhere),

Yellow warbler on the pier in Puerto Ayora, Santa Cruz

twenty-seven regular migrants, and sixty-seven "vagrant" or "accidental."

If you are a dedicated birder, the chance to add perhaps twenty of the forty-four endemic species to your life list is one of the great draws of the trip. The islands are also home to a large number of the other resident birds, some of which are rarely seen anywhere else in their range. Birders and nonbirders alike will have the opportunity to see the birdlife up close for extended periods. The times you spend on a boat—whether a week-long tour, a day trip from one of the communities, or an island-hopping few days—will give you a very good chance to see an array of oceangoing (pelagic) birds. Petrels dance on the waters, boobies dive after schools of fish, frigates soar above.

On land, as you carefully follow your naturalist guide along the paths, there will be the Darwin's finches to try to sort out. There are fifteen species in all, fourteen on the islands, including a warbler that has now been classified as a finch, and the fifteenth being another very closely related one that is found on Cocos Island, in the Pacific Ocean, 540 kilometers (340 miles) off the coast of Costa Rica. But numbers aside, it is simply wonderful to see the fine gradations of size and shape and to hear the slight variations of their vocalizations. On my first visit, in 1981, while on Santa Cruz, I actually saw a woodpecker finch grasp a cactus thorn in its beak and use it to pry an insect out of a tree cactus—tool use in birds!

There will be mockingbirds brashly flying over you, or walking along the beach—they are omnivorous and feed in a variety of habitats. There is one distinct species of mockingbird found on each of Floreana, San Cristóbal, and Española islands. You may see the brilliantly colorful yellow warbler, seeming often to be picking at insects caught in the debris at the edge of waves on a sandy beach. Or the Galapagos flycatcher flitting just above your head as it snaps at an insect, or if you're really fortunate, a vermilion flycatcher may dart above you. Different species of herons are in their favorite habitats, though they range widely across the islands. Watch for migrants, also. For each of my trips I've seen whimbrels and semipalmated plovers, sandpipers, and willets.

There are also several fairly recently introduced bird species, which have become well established. Two species that can be readily seen especially around human habitation are the smooth-billed ani and the cattle egret (both noted as early as the 1960s). The egrets were likely introduced to control pests on cattle. They seem to be quite benign in their sharing of space and food with other bird and animal life. However, it is different for the anis, which are very aggressive birds. They are being monitored by the Park Service in case their presence on certain islands begins to heavily affect small land birds, such as the finches, as food competitors and predators of eggs or nestlings.

Not only is it easy to see many of the land and seabird species found in the islands, it is often possible to see them busily engaged in nesting. The equator does not have the clearly differentiated seasons of more temperate latitudes. The length of day is constant, and there are no strong light-related cues to set hormones racing and mate searching for mate. Temperatures on the islands are nearly constant, although in El Niño years both air and water temperatures can soar. There are wet and dry seasons, but they are ill-defined and not entirely predictable. The wet season lasts from December to May, and the dry or *garua* season lasts from June to November. The effects of climate change on the oceans and the food sources within them also affect the nesting opportunities of many of the pelagic birds. There are signs that some of the primary fish species, such as sardines, are in rapid and serious decline, which can have negative effects on the reproductive success of birds such as the various boobies.

There are active research projects monitoring the status of wildlife, to identify where changes in food supplies and reproductive patterns may be attributed to changes in water and land temperatures related to climate change. Climate change and the effects on plant life, on the shifting success of plants on which land and seabirds depend, are also a continuing focus of research and management to address these

Great frigate bird in a deflated moment, Genovesa

conditions. All of these factors mean that food supplies may fluctuate, which affects the survival rate of land and seabirds. This relates to their reproductive success as well.

For the visitor, there are always fascinating birds to be seen, birds that you may see only once in a lifetime. Depending on your itinerary, the avian breeding patterns, and the time of year you are there, you may be able to walk at a respectful distance from the flightless cormorant at its nest, or follow paths taking you alongside a frigate bird nesting site, as they puff out their red pouches and warble and flap their wings to attract females. There may be the opportunity to walk among nesting

Nazca boobies, or the very large and quite ungainly waved albatross.

Seabirds

Nineteen seabird species breed in the islands, and six of these are endemic. The endemic ones are spectacular. There is the Galapagos penguin (*Spheniscus mendiculus*), a type of bird we usually associate with the colder world regions like the Antarctic, the southern tip of South America or the southern shore of Australia. But here under the blast of the equatorial sun we can see this unique species carrying out its everyday life.

An innovative project began in 2010 to build shady nest sites on three major islands (Isabela, Fernandina, and Bartolomé) where penguins currently breed. The nests are constructed out of natural materials such as lava rocks and placed in crevices and gaps along the rocky edges of these islands. The biologists monitor them several times a year to determine if artificial nest sites do, in fact, increase reproduction and reproductive success when food is available. The hope is that this project will stop the decline in the Galapagos penguin population, and that the population will be strengthened so that it can better withstand the impacts of the climate fluctuations caused by more frequent El Niño events.

The flightless cormorant (*Phalacrocorax harrisi*) is also endemic. It is an eerily prehistoric-looking bird, with its reptilian neck and head. When not slipping in and out of the water to fish, these cormorants often stand very still, their disproportionately small wings outspread. Like others in their family, their feathers have little protective oil. This means that their feathers do not repel the seawater to any great degree and the birds must hang their wings out to dry after any feeding sortie. The wings are too small for flight in the air, but wonderful for underwater flight, propelled by their webbed feet which are set far to the end of their body. The cormorants do have a small oil gland on the base of their tail, which they dip into for preening, although it does not serve to make them waterproof. But they do not get waterlogged in their deep dives,

because they have very dense, almost downlike feathers and these trap tiny air bubbles, which allows them to dive, swim, feed, and pop up to the surface to return to their rocky home and start the drying process again.

The waved albatross (*Phoebastria irrorata*) is considered endemic, though there are a very few pairs nesting on an island near the coast of Ecuador (and the viability and status of these few is very uncertain). This magnificent bird is classified as *critically endangered* by the International Union for Conservation of Nature, as defined in its Red List (see the appendix) because of its very small breeding range—only on Española. It appears to be experiencing a significant decline in numbers, which is attributed largely to fishing practices such as long-lining, where the birds can be trapped in the miles of nets and hooks that are used in industrial fishing out in the Pacific far from the safety of the Galapagos Marine Reserve. The albatross nests in Galapagos but forages as far afield as the coasts of Peru, a very active commercial fishing ground.

The beautiful swallow-tailed gull (*Creagrus furcatus*) is very distinctive for being largely nocturnal in its feeding and activity patterns. It feeds on squid and other fish that are near the surface of the sea. This gull is not considered to be a particularly vulnerable or threatened species. The gulls nest in a variety of situations, from gravelly, flat, open spaces to rocky cliff edges and even near the shoreline. They don't have a specific nesting season, but will gather in groups here and there to nest, while another group may nest at another time in the year. Their nest is just a scrape in the surrounding sticks, dust, and small rocks. The chicks have the superb camouflage characteristic of field-nesters (like so many shorebirds around the world), and it is particularly important to walk carefully in the visitor sites that include nesting pairs. Visitors may have set paths, but the gulls don't read signs. Though considered to be endemic to the Galapagos, there are a very few that nest on an island off the coast of Colombia.

The uniformly gray lava gulls are few in number, but you still are likely to see this endemic species as you come and go to various visitor sites, or one may sit for a few minutes on your boat now and then. They don't breed in groups like the swallow-tailed gull, and seem to be much more reclusive, especially when nesting. They eat a wide range of food, including the eggs of other seabirds, young marine iguanas, and small fish or crustaceans. They are also a regular visitor at the fish market in Puerto Ayora, on Santa Cruz Island. Their numbers are estimated to be only about one thousand individuals, though a firm count has not been made. But because of these small numbers, they are classified as *vulnerable*.

The sixth endemic seabird is the Galapagos petrel (*Pterodroma phaeopygia*). They can be seen soaring near the surface of the sea, with a swooping arc of many meters. The white forehead and the white shading extending from the belly along the underside of the wings make it easy to identify. These seabirds nest in the highlands of the five larger islands—Santa Cruz, Floreana, Santiago, San Cristóbal, and Isabela. They nest in burrows or natural cavities, often on hillsides. This nesting pattern, of course, made them very vulnerable to introduced predators like rats and cats, loss of their habitat, and also to being crushed by the hooves of cattle or horses. They were approaching extinction on the islands, but there have been real successes in reducing or eradicating feral predators, with more protection against agriculturally based threats. However, the Galapagos petrel is still rated as *critically endangered* because of the low population, with so many risks to their survival still existing.

Many of the other seabirds are quite dramatic in their own ways. There are the huge and somehow ominous frigate birds (*Fregata minor* and *F. magnificens*), which are described as klepto-parasites because they live off other seabirds by stealing their food. Like the cormorants, frigates have only a very small oil gland and diving for food is not an option. Thus, robbing from others that can dive is a successful adaptation—for the frigates. You can often see frigates harassing a lava gull or booby with a fish in its beak. Suddenly, after an avian dogfight, the smaller bird drops the fish and the frigate bird swoops down to snatch the morsel before it hits the water. It can do this even if it is flying several meters above the other bird. If by chance the food hits the water and sinks more than a few centimeters before the frigate bird gets to it, the frigate bird abandons the quest and another chase may soon be on.

Other birds of open water are the Nazca (*Sula granti*) and blue-footed boobies (*S. nebouxii*). The blue-footed booby is seen very often because it hunts fish in the shallow sea near the shores, where the tour boats spend much of their time. The Nazca booby fishes much farther out to sea, so it is usually seen at its nests on islands such as Daphne Major, Genovesa, or Española. However, according to recent research the drastic diminution of sardine stocks—a core part of the blue-footed booby diet—is causing concern. Fewer boobies are being seen, and breeding appears to be drastically reduced. To be able to breed, a bird (or any other creature) must have enough food for its body to generate the signals to reproduce—to form pairs, have offspring, and care for them until they are able to survive on their own. The loss of sardine stocks can be associated with climate change, in that even a slight increase in ocean temperature, or degrees of acidification, can reduce the viability of the plankton on which fish such as sardines rely.

Many of the seabirds are ground nesters; some of these, such as the petrels, nest in burrows. This includes the Galapagos shearwater (*Puffinus subalaris*).

Swallow-tailed gull chick, shaded by one of its parents, Genovesa

The red-billed tropicbird (*Phaethon aethereus*) nests in the rocky crevices of several islands. The brown noddy (*Anous stolidus*) nests on cliffs by the sea and in small caves. The blue-footed booby nests on the open ground on a number of the islands; some can still be seen nesting on Seymour Norte, the cliff sides of Daphne Major, and on Española. Their mating behavior is a charming and amusing sight as they paddle their bright blue webbed feet up and down, throwing their wings out and head and tail up, wheezing all the while.

But the red-footed booby (*Sula sula*) actually nests in trees and shrubs. They can be seen on Genovesa, peering down on visitors from their rather shaky vantage points.

White phase of red-footed booby, Genovesa

Look for the toenails that help them keep a grip on the windblown branches they cling to. The other shrub- or tree-nesting (it's hard to tell sometimes where a shrub leaves off and a tree begins in the islands) birds are both frigate bird species and the pelican (*Pelecanus occidentalis*). Even if these are seabirds, you don't have to be at sea to see many of them. Just in walking around towns, perhaps going to one of the coves here and there, you can often see boobies or frigates. And you certainly can see pelicans at the local fish markets!

Land Birds

Just as the seabirds rely on the sea for their food supply, the land birds rely on

the food found on the landmasses. In very general terms, the land birds follow the vegetation zones of the islands because the different plants supply the range of food used by different species. However, the division of birds into sea and land leaves out the birds that spend much of their time on the edges of the land while feeding in the shallows of the sea, the lagoons, and the few ponds and lakes of the islands. Among these are the Galapagos gallinule (*Gallinula chloropus*, or "coot"), the flamingo (*Phoenicopterus ruber*), five members of the heron family, the white-cheeked pintail duck (*Anas bahamensis*), and two shorebirds, the American oystercatcher (*Haematopus palliatus*) and the common stilt (*Himantopus mexicanus*).

Be alert in the mangrove lagoons for the striated herons, for great blue herons along the rocks at the water's edge, for lava herons along the rocks of the port of San Cristóbal, for the yellow-crowned night heron in the fur seal grottoes. I've seen one of the latter there on every one of my trips. I like to think it's been waiting for me.

Aside from the birds living mostly along the shore and in the mangroves, twenty-nine land bird species breed on the Galapagos. All but two of them are endemic, a very large proportion of the whole avian repertoire of the islands. In types they range from the endemic Galapagos hawk (*Buteo galapagoensis*) to two members of the rail family that live in the moist, dense highlands of several islands, an endemic dove (*Zenaida galapagoensis*), a cuckoo, two owl species, two flycatchers, one warbler, four mockingbirds, and the fourteen species of the Darwin's finches. Many of the bird populations are in a precarious state. The vermilion flycatcher appears to have disappeared from the populated islands of Floreana and San Cristóbal; there is still hope for populations on other islands. Several iconic land bird populations are in a spiraling decline. Mangrove and medium tree finches, as well as the Floreana mockingbird, are all rated as *critically endangered*. Timely studies of these species, as well as vermilion flycatchers, may prevent

the first extinction of a bird species in Galapagos since humans first discovered the islands.

In the face of this dire situation, the survival of the mangrove finch (*Camarhynchus heliobates*) provides a truly inspiring example of an effort to halt imminent extinction of a species. As of 2013, there were only sixty to eighty mangrove finches left in existence. They could be found in two large mangrove forests on the western coast of Isabela Island. They nest and live their daily lives among the tallest of the mangrove trees.

In 2013, researchers from the Charles Darwin Foundation and the San Diego Zoo Global collaborated to establish a captive

Galapagos hawk, Santiago

Oystercatchers preening, Española

rearing program for mangrove finches in an attempt to begin to restore their population. The primary threat to the mangrove finch is the invasive avian parasite *Philornis downsi*, which lays its eggs in the nests of finches. *Philornis* larvae then feed on the tissue and blood of nestlings, causing high mortality among the young birds.

In early February 2014, twenty-one eggs and three newly hatched chicks were collected from wild nests in the mangrove forest on Isabela and transported to the newly created incubation and hand-rearing facility at the Charles Darwin Research Station. This is a quarantine facility, so the risk of infection by the *P. downsi* larvae is greatly reduced. In March 2014, when the hand-rearing process was complete (which takes as many as fifteen hand-feedings a day), ten of the young birds were returned to an aviary on western Isabela before being released back into the mangrove forest and monitored by the field team. After several weeks in the aviary the birds were released. Each has a tiny transmitter attached, to allow for monitoring. The foundation continued this successful species recovery program for a second year in 2015. Your guide should be able to update you on the program's progress.

A trip of at least one week should allow you to see the great majority of the land birds. It will be difficult to locate and identify each of the Darwin's finches, but with a good guide on board and careful attention to your bird guidebook, you should be able to see at least half of them. In any case, it will be very clear that they are different in size, beak shape, and behavior.

MAMMALS

The mammals of the Galapagos can be grouped according to whether they depend on the sea or the land for food. One further distinction is that between the native and the introduced species. The latter are more numerous in types and in absolute numbers, and they play a very different role in the islands than do the native mammals.

Marine Mammals

Two marine mammals breed and live much of their lives in the islands. Both are endemic and of the eared seal family:

the sea lion (*Zalophus wollebaeki*) and the fur seal (*Arctocephalus galapagoensis*).

The sea lion, often seen by visitors, is by far the larger of the two, with the mature males weighing as much as 250 kilograms (550 pounds). The females are appreciably smaller but still very sturdy. Sea lions congregate in groups of females and their pups, with a bull sea lion patrolling the territory that his family group occupies. These territorial groupings are highly fluid and stay under the sway of a particular male for only two weeks or so.

There are several accessible sea lion nurseries, or *loberias*. These include Caamaño Islet near Puerto Ayora, the beachfront of Puerto Baquerizo Moreno on San Cristóbal, and on Floreana.

Younger males who do not have their own territories gather in what are called

Nursing baby sea lion, Santiago

Common dolphins, often seen around the southern islands

bachelor groups. As they grow older and more assertive they are able to establish their own relationships with females and set up their own territories. They may do this by raiding an existent group when the leading male is off feeding or squabbling with another male.

Sea lions are very active during the day, especially in the morning and in the late afternoon. They congregate in large numbers on sandy beaches, open rocky shores, or areas a few dozen meters (over one hundred feet) inland but with easy access to the water.

Pups are born most months of the year except April and May. This means that a visitor has a very good chance of seeing pups suckling noisily or playing in the waves. When you are swimming, it is not uncommon to have these curious creatures swooshing right next to you.

Even though the sea lions are certainly a feature of your visit, populations have declined, from an estimated forty thousand since the 1970s, to present estimates of around fifteen thousand. The sea lion is now listed as *endangered*. Here again is the link between climate change and species loss, in that the sea is the source of the sea lion's food, and warmer water temperatures diminish food supplies. Less food means fewer of these playful, fascinating mammals.

The Galapagos fur seal is the smallest of the fur seals found in the southern hemisphere, and it is the only one that lives in tropical waters. Unlike other fur seals, it does not spend most of its time in the water, migrating from one area to another for food or for breeding. These seals spend their lives around the archipelago, with about 30 percent of their time being spent on land. They have a number of strategies for withstanding the extreme heat and dryness of the coastal zone. For example, they spend much of their day in the cool of rocky shores and cliffs, where they can get out of the sun. They also feed mostly at night, catching squid and fish.

There are estimated to be about eight thousand fur seals in the islands. Populations have declined from an estimated thirty to forty thousand since the 1970s, and the fur seal is listed as *endangered*. They breed on most of the islands and can be found on or around most of them. They have their pups between June and December, which tends to be the cooler time of year and the time of the greater food supply.

Visitors do not see the fur seal nearly as regularly as they do the sea lion, but at one or two sites, such as the fur seal grottoes on Santiago, there are excellent opportunities to view them up close.

Other marine mammals can be seen in the Galapagos, but they are not land-based for breeding and other activities, as are the sea lion and fur seal. These other marine mammals are the whales, dolphins, and porpoises that frequent the waters of the archipelago. Most commonly the visitor will see the bottle-nosed dolphin (*Tursiops truncatus*) racing alongside the boat or even riding the bow waves. It is easy to photograph them because they may accompany a boat for many minutes at a time. (Use a polarizing filter if you have one.)

Whales, such as the humpback and orca (killer whale), are seen less often, but a lucky visitor may spot them.

Land Mammals

Land mammals are less able to make the long and dangerous trip to far-flung islands; thus it is not surprising that the (surviving) native mammals include two flying ones (bats) and four rat species.

Rats are among the most resilient of all animals and evidently could survive the trip on the mats of vegetable matter that are assumed to have drifted from mainland Ecuador to the islands. A dense mat of vegetation only a few meters square would provide them with enough shade, moisture, and food to make the trip. Of course, humans have brought rats with them for centuries.

Evidence suggests there were once twelve rat species native to the islands. However, the introduced black rat has all but obliterated the native rats. The rediscovery in 1998 of the endemic Santiago rice rat was an exciting surprise, as it was believed to be extinct for over a century. Visitors are not likely to see the endemic rats, except on Santa Fe where the Santa Fe rice rat (*Oryzomys bauri*) can be seen scurrying about. Major efforts are underway to eliminate the introduced rats from the Galapagos. They are already gone from Seymour Norte, and eradication work is underway on Rábida. As noted earlier, as of 2012, rats have also been eradicated from Pinzon. Perhaps one day rats will no longer threaten the fragile plant and animal life on these islands.

There are two species of bat in the islands, though there is not much known about them at this time. One, the hoary bat (*Lasiurus cinereus*), is widely distributed in both North and South America. It is an insect eater, and it roosts in mangrove trees or other lowland bush during the day. It is found on five of the islands: Santa Cruz, San Cristóbal, Isabela, Santiago, and Floreana. The other bat, *Lasiurus brachyotis*, is endemic. It is an inhabitant of the highlands and coastal areas of Santa Cruz. It feeds on insect life that feeds near the ground, swooping down at night to capture its prey in flight. Because of their different feeding and roosting patterns, these two bats seem not to compete for territory or food.

The introduced mammals, such as goats, dogs, cats, and other domestic animals, have been discussed earlier in terms of their negative impact on the environment of the islands. Their different and highly predatory modes of feeding and breeding and their caution around humans make nonnative mammals a uniformly destructive segment of the mammal population. Stopping more introduced species from arriving and spreading, and controlling or eliminating those already here are top priorities. Your visit to the Galapagos will certainly increase your awareness of the complexities of the ecosystem and the daunting nature of restoring threatened and endangered island life-forms.

REPTILES

The most well-known reptiles on these islands are, of course, the giant tortoises, with their variously shaped backs, their vital history to the islands, their importance currently to scientific research, and their value as a source of fascination for visitors. Then there are the iguanas, the marine-based ones, shiny black, basking on the rocks, slipping into the water to feed on some seaweed. Large and surprisingly colorful, the land iguanas vary from island to island. Watching them gnaw on prickly pear spines is a startling experience in itself! As for snakes, I was lucky enough to see one, once. They don't loom large in the legends of the islands, but keep your eyes open.

Tortoises

The iconic animal of the Galapagos Islands is the giant tortoise (*Chelonoidis*), with ten species of the original fourteen still existent, though genetic research is now distinguishing some subspecies.

The giant tortoises can weigh 300 kilograms (660 pounds) and measure 150 centimeters (60 inches) across the shell. The largest ever recorded, from Alcedo volcano on Isabela, weighed in at 319 kilograms (703 pounds). They look slow and awkward, but they can move quite rapidly and are amazingly flexible in their movements. The most obvious way to distinguish a particular race from the others is by the size and the shape of the shell, or carapace. The relatively smaller ones (with a saddleback shape) are found on Española and Pinta, and the largest (dome-shaped) ones are found on Santa Cruz and Isabela's Alcedo volcano. The others range between these two ends of the size spectrum.

One very unusual shell, apparently a squashed dome shell, is only found in one subpopulation, from the Cinco Cerros area on Isabela. It is now being bred in captivity. This subpopulation has a very interesting history of a narrow escape from disaster and possible extinction. Locally it is known as *aplastada* (flattened) because of the peculiar shape of its shell. In 1994 it was estimated that there were approximately seventy aplastadas in their home range. The main reason for this low number apparently was strong nest predation by ants of the genus *Solenopsis* (which include fire ants, a scourge in many places in the islands).

In September 1998, the eruption of Cerro Azul volcano threatened to burn the area where this very rare subpopulation was concentrated. Due to the emergency of the situation, and with the assistance of the Ecuadorean Army, an air evacuation of these tortoises was carried out. The rescued animals were moved to the Rearing Center in Puerto Villamil, on Isabela, which had only two of these tortoises. Breeding success has brought the number, as of 2014, to seventeen: seven males and ten females. Your guide should be able to update you on their most recent numbers.

Over the centuries the giant tortoises have suffered terribly from the direct predations of people, from buccaneers to explorers to farmers and other island occupants. Even today, poaching remains a problem, and authorities continue to combat it. Tortoises have also suffered from the indirect impact of people. Introduced grazing mammals such as goats and burros outcompeted them for food and destroyed their habitat. And because tortoises lay their eggs in the ground, the eggs and hatchlings are eaten by rats or are trampled by burros. With all those attacks on their existence, the results are hardly surprising. There were once hundreds of thousands of tortoises on the islands; there are now somewhat more than twenty-five thousand.

The greatest known surviving concentrations are on Alcedo volcano and Darwin volcano on Isabela and in the highlands of Santa Cruz and San Cristóbal. It is on walks to these highlands that you are most likely to see them in their natural state. You will be able to see the hatchlings and some of the adults at the Park Service Tortoise Centers on San Cristóbal, Isabela, and Santa Cruz. With the loss of the last of the Pinta Island tortoises, Lonesome George, in 2012, it was thought that his species was then extinct. Very recently, with advances in genetic research, scientists have learned that there are tortoises on Isabela's Wolf volcano that are related to the Pinta tortoise. It is hoped that by captive breeding, with selected pairings of individuals with the related genetic components, it will be possible for Lonesome George's genetic life line to be reestablished. If scientists were able to do so, these would be returned to Pinta, once again to play their crucial part in sustaining the complex environment there.

At the two tortoise breeding centers, on Santa Cruz and San Cristóbal, you have a wonderful view of the tortoises that are being raised as part of the restoration effort. It's great to see the tortoises up close like that, from tiny ones barely a month old to huge mature adults.

The establishment of the Galapagos National Park Directorate and the combined work of the Park Service and the Charles Darwin Foundation can be credited with saving the giant tortoise species and individuals that remain. Today nine of the ten remaining species range from *vulnerable* to *critically endangered*. Yet in spite of habitat restoration and captive breeding, the tortoises face great challenges to be able to increase in substantial numbers in their natural environment. They must still be very carefully reared, returned to their original island where possible, and monitored and protected on their home territory. They have to reach a size where they cannot be eaten or crushed, and this means they will be usually around four years old before they are released to the wild. They do not reach sexual maturity until about thirty years old, which means a long, slow process of

successful restoration and return to their home territories.

At the same time, the efforts continue to reduce habitat deterioration and to repair and regenerate the home islands to their original state. There is no point returning the tortoises if their food supply is uncertain or inadequate. Life is a web, after all, and a tear in one part of it will shred other parts—and repair to all, at the same time, is crucial to survival of the whole.

Sea Turtles

Several species of sea turtle also occur widely in the surrounding waters, including the loggerhead sea turtle (*Caretta caretta*) and the East Pacific green turtle (*Chelonia mydas agassisi*).

The East Pacific green turtle breeds in a number of the lagoons of the islands. (You may well see a pair coupled as they slowly swim in a lagoon.) After mating, the females lay their eggs in the sand of several island beaches. This mode of reproduction leaves the turtles very vulnerable to predation. Introduced rats destroy nests and eat eggs, and hatchlings making their way to the sea are taken by native predators such as hawks, herons, mockingbirds, and frigate birds. The Park Service and the guides are very careful to make sure that paths or open beaches are identified as nesting sites and to ensure that visitors not tread in these areas. Once the hatchlings reach the sea, sharks and fish prey on them. Those that do

A marine iguana's ugly beauty, Española

make it to open water safely and survive for the next several years will return to the lagoons and beaches of their origin and reproduce as best they can there. One of the most likely sites to see these turtles during their mating activities is at Caleta Tortuga Negra on Santa Cruz.

Iguanas

Almost as well-known as the giant tortoise and the sea turtles are the iguanas, marine and land, of the Galapagos. Much less well-known are the seven lizard species, three snake species, and seven gecko species. You will see several of the lizard species, but are unlikely to see the snakes or geckos. It's really a matter of luck.

The iguanas of the islands are very striking in both looks and behavior. They are members of the lizard family. The best known and most commonly seen is the endemic marine iguana (*Amblyrhynchus cristatus*). It is the only truly marine lizard in the world. These iguanas can reach a length of 100 centimeters (40 inches) and weigh as much as 8 kilograms (17.6 pounds). Genetic studies revealed the existence of a particularly distinctive marine iguana population, known as the Punta Pitt iguanas, from their location on San Cristóbal. That singular population appears to be very few in number and may be in urgent need of conservation management due to the risk of predation from feral cats.

Marine iguanas are also heavily affected by extreme weather events, such as the 1997–98 El Niño; at that time 90 percent of some populations were lost. However, the marine iguanas seem to recover quickly and are presently very numerous. While the total population is not known, the International Union for the Conservation of Nature suggests that there are at least fifty thousand marine iguanas on the islands, but estimates from the Charles Darwin Research Station are in the hundreds of thousands.

No matter which number is close, you can be sure of seeing marine iguanas in many places during your visit. They spend much of their time resting in large groups on rocky shores, but also can be seen wandering around the waterfronts of towns, like the fish market in Puerto Ayora or the waterfront walkway of Puerto Baquerizo Moreno on San Cristóbal. Wherever they are, the marine iguanas love to sit soaking up the sun, sending out occasional puffs through their nostrils of salty residue from ingested seawater. They will drink fresh water when it is around, and I observed one along the waterfront in San Cristóbal descend from its resting place on a rustic fence to lap up water in a recently created rain puddle. But when they need to eat, the females and younger iguanas leave their perches and swim to nearby patches of seaweed and graze on them. The stronger males are able to swim farther out to sea to feed.

Their preferred food is algae, which can disappear during an El Niño event, causing massive die-off of these iguanas. Researchers have found, however, that some marine iguanas are able to adjust to this extreme situation by reducing their skeletal size, a change most likely triggered by a stress hormone. When food supplies return to a plentiful level, those iguanas apparently return to their normal length.

Marine iguanas are ground-nesting animals, the female laying eggs in the burrow she has dug. Unlike the sea turtles, the females stay around their nests for a week or so to guard them from predators. Of course, even with the guarding activity, the nests and hatchlings are subject to the same sorts of predation as those of the sea turtles.

There are seven subspecies of marine iguana on the islands. You can see clearly how they differ in size and appearance in some locations. For example, the iguanas near the fur seal grottoes on Santiago are much smaller and more uniformly black than the larger ones of Española, which have great splashes of deep red on their sides.

There are three land iguana species on the islands (*Conolophus subcristatus*, *C. marthae*, and *C. pallidus*), all of which are endemic. They, too, are quite different in looks and habits from their marine counterparts. They tend to be solitary, unlike the highly gregarious marine iguanas. They are much bulkier than the marine iguanas, which are quite sleek by comparison. The land iguanas are generally

LEFT: *Land iguana, Santa Cruz* RIGHT: *Female lava lizard, Española*

yellow, with brown or black shading on the back ridge. The species *C. pallidus* is found only on Santa Fe. *C. subcristatus* is found on Fernandina (which has the largest population of them), Isabela, Santa Cruz, Baltra, Seymour Norte, and Plaza Sur where the latter species is often seen dotting the landscape like huge yellow flowers. They feed there on the succulent ground cover, *Portulaca oleracea*, and gnaw through the spiny paddles of the *Opuntia* cactus without any hesitation.

The small population of around five hundred "pink iguanas" (*Conolophus marthae*), found only along the rim of the crater of Wolf volcano on Isabela, was described in 2009. To have found such a large new species is an indicator of how much more there is still to be discovered on these enchanted islands.

On visits to Santa Fe, your guide usually can find some *C. pallidus* individuals. They are few in number but wonderful to see. They are a paler yellow than the other land iguana species, with a more tapered snout, and the spiky ridges along their back are heavier. Mostly they are just splayed out in the dust, blinking occasionally at the visitors peering down at them.

Other Reptiles

There are lava lizards (*Tropidurus* spp.) on most of the main islands, a frequent sight for visitors. There are seven subspecies, all of them endemic, varying in size and color from island to island. The lava lizards average about 25 centimeters (10 inches) and are generally grayish brown, some with subtle striping over the head

Blue sea star—snorkeling bonus

Jeroen Nijénstein and Eva Mulder

and body. One of their outstanding features is that mature females have a bright patch of red on the throat and cheeks. They will perch on the top of a rock, pumping their little bodies up and down as though doing reptilian push-ups. Lava lizards feed on a variety of insects, spiders, and even snails.

The geckos are not well-known and are seldom seen. One obvious reason is that they are nocturnal, so visitors would have little opportunity to see them. There are seven species, all endemic. Several introduced geckos are quickly displacing the native in inhabited areas. They also are threatened by rats, though rat eradication on Rábida seems to have left room for an endemic gecko, discovered in 2011.

The terrestrial snakes of the Galapagos, all nonpoisonous constrictors, are seen occasionally by visitors. There are three genera and four species of snakes. They are up to around a meter (3 feet) long when fully grown, and feed on lava lizards, marine iguana hatchlings, and some bird nestlings. In turn, the snakes are preyed on by feral cats and the Galapagos hawk. Very unusual behavior has been documented on Fernandina where the constrictor endemic to the area prefers to hunt small fish trapped in the tidepools when the tide goes out.

MARINE LIFE

The establishment of the Marine Reserve component of the Galapagos National Park has created greater opportunities for visitation, scientific research, and protection of this largest single habitat in the islands. It is astonishingly rich and varied, and it shapes the quality of all other life in the archipelago.

With the creation of the reserve and the establishment of around seventy-five marine visitor sites, you will have many opportunities to snorkel. This development has dramatically expanded the Galapagos experience. Visitors have the chance to enjoy and learn while immersed.

Currents and Temperature

The Galapagos are at the convergence of three major oceanic currents—the north equatorial, the equatorial (Cromwell), and the Humboldt (Peru) coastal currents. This puts the islands at the meeting of great underwater rivers that have differing temperatures, lateral and vertical directions, and a wide range of kinds and amounts of plants and animals. The rivers also have varying chemical profiles. All of this adds up to an extremely rich environment that is home to an unimaginable array of marine life.

Yet the negative impacts of climate change, the increased temperature of the oceans as a whole, its acidification, and contamination through waste dumping, oil spills, and other events and sources that are reducing that richness and diversity across the planet, are also being felt in the Galapagos. Even within this negative trend, it still is the case that the waters surrounding the islands exhibit

the same high proportion of endemic species as does the land. Plant life in the surrounding waters has been estimated to include about 360 species, with 16 percent endemic. There are an estimated eight hundred mollusk species, of which 17 percent are endemic. There are also twenty-four sea urchin species, twenty-eight sea stars, and thirty sea cucumber species.

The generally cool waters and concomitant dryness of the land occasionally are interrupted by a current of warm water that is unusual in that it swings away from its ordinary path on the west coast of Central America. When this current, known as El Niño (or ENSO, El Niño Southern Oscillation), reaches the Galapagos, it causes temporary but drastic changes in the ocean life, in the lives of animals that depend on the ocean for food, and in the weather and everyday life of all the plants and animals of the islands.

The El Niño current is a very warm mass of water. Warm water is nutrient poor. It holds less oxygen than an equivalent volume of cold water, and with less oxygen there is less underwater plant life (phytoplankton). Less plant life means less food for marine animal life, from the tiniest crustacean to the biggest shark or whale. Less marine animal life means less food for seagoing mammals and birds. All of these factors converge during El Niño events.

In El Niño years the average water temperature soars from its usual 16°C (71°F)

Sally Lightfoot crab feeling for food, Santa Cruz

to 20°C (68°F) to nearly 30°C (86°F). The effect on all sea life is dramatic. The changes in surface temperatures and weather also are enormous. The islands are inundated with downpours. Land is washed away. Plants blossom that haven't done so for years. Seabirds may have so little food that they do not even attempt to nest. Sea lion and fur seal colonies may succeed in raising only very few young, if any. Marine iguanas die when the algae they feed on disappears because it is unable to grow in the warmer waters. By

contrast, land birds such as the finches may find themselves with so much food that they raise four or five broods over just a few months.

Until recently, it seemed that a strong El Niño event came only every thirteen years or so, with milder events occurring more frequently every few years. The opposite of an El Niño is La Niña, a time of reduced moisture on land. This also has been occurring more frequently. A great deal of research is being done to determine the effects of these two types of oceanic events. An El Niño is nothing new to the islands, and as devastating as it may seem, most life bounces back very quickly. However, there are concerns that the recent trends in the frequency of these currents will make it more difficult for plants and animals to recover if they are hit again with such an event within three or four years. In this case, the endemic species can be at an even greater disadvantage in the competition with introduced plants and animals.

Exploring the Marine World

For the typical visitor, some of this marine life can be seen when snorkeling, although more and more divers are enjoying this beautiful undersea world. The life of the intertidal zone (the areas at the water's edge that appear and disappear with the tides) is very evident to any visitor, however. The most obvious residents of these wave-splashed areas are the crabs. The Sally Lightfoot (*Grapsus grapsus*) is one of a hundred crab species in the islands, but its size and brilliant reds and purples make it the most easily seen. The younger ones are nearly black like the lava they walk across, but the older ones, which reach the size of a human hand, become a bright orange that really stands out in contrast to the black lava rocks they so often haunt.

In contrast to the striking coloration and size of the Sally Lightfoot crab is the ghost crab (*Ocypode albicans*). Its name comes from its pale, almost translucent

coloring, which can make it hard to pick out as it scuttles along the sand. We saw thousands of them once, on the beautiful beach at the east side of Floreana's Punta Cormorán. They are only a few centimeters in size but well worth a look if you can get close enough to one.

With the growing emphasis on exploring the marine life of the islands, tour boats generally have the basic equipment for snorkeling. This is easy to do if the water is calm, and even a few minutes can give a very strong sense of the variety and beauty of the marine life. You can also scuba dive in the islands. There are live-aboard boats that specialize in this service, with their own scuba-licensed guides and support equipment. In case of emergency there is a hyperbaric chamber in Puerto Ayora. Guides in some of the communities offer day trips. If you decide to take this option, in arranging to go, make sure all personnel and equipment are fully certified.

Effects of the Expansion of the Marine Environment

It is interesting to see how the inclusion and subsequent expansion into the national park itself of the marine environment affects both the underwater life itself and the experience of the visitor, not to mention the residents of the islands and international commercial fishing companies. The commercial use of the marine resources, such as sea cucumbers, has been a very contentious issue, calling for every bit of negotiating and management skill available in the Galapagos Islands, the Ecuadorean government, and the international environmental community. The sea cucumber is now considered to be commercially extinct, and for several years there has been a moratorium on fishing them. Lobster fishing is also strictly regulated. Meanwhile, you as a visitor are likely to find plenty of time to become acquainted with the marvels of the marine life of the islands.

The marine life of the Galapagos has been little studied in comparison to land research. The creation of the expanded marine reserve in 1998 was based on increased research in the preceding years, as the impacts of expanded fishing and tourism became ever more apparent. In 2002, the first baseline survey of the marine reserve area was published. In 2012 the first studies on marine invasive species began with the discovery of an introduced alga.

Over the past few years there has been a great increase in the recognition of the risks to the marine environment of introduced species. Attention was paid to the risks to the land and its life-forms, whether from human activities, volcanic activity, or climate change. But now efforts are well underway to identify the kinds and numbers of introduced marine species, to determine their threat to the marine environment (with implications for the land, of course), and to reduce or prevent their introduction and negative impacts.

Authorities are applying much stricter controls on movement into and between islands, by recreational or commercial vessels. Visiting private ships might find themselves sent out of the Marine Reserve if their hull is not clean. Introduced corals, barnacles, even viruses or bacteria from dumped ballast, not to speak of possible fuel spills or illegally jettisoned garbage, all can contaminate the water, damage underwater plant and animal life, or displace life-forms by outcompeting them for food, living space, or reproductive opportunities.

Opposite: *Blue-footed booby overlooking Daphne Major*

PART II

PLANNING YOUR
GALAPAGOS TRIP

The Galapagos Islands are a very special place, with diverse environments and many different ways of experiencing them. The section that follows is designed to help you plan a trip to the islands with recommendations on what to bring, along with notes on photography and access for persons with mobility limitations. Then, part III of this book will take you to most of the sites where you are likely to go.

First, the trip to the islands is a long way from almost anywhere, even for Ecuadoreans who fly or sail the 1000 kilometers (620 miles) from the mainland to get there. The way plane travel has changed in the last decade, it is usual for the trip to Quito (or Guayaquil) from most locations around the world to take at least 24 hours. When scheduling your trip, it is essential that you allow yourself at least another 24 hours to stay in either of the arrival cities before the planned departure for the islands themselves. As you'll see in the next chapter, I suggest you spend several days in Quito and another couple of weeks on the Ecuador mainland, in the highlands and rain forest. But if you are going to the Galapagos only, you still do not want to worry about missing your next flight because you assumed that you could simply have a brief stopover in Quito or Guayaquil and hop on the next plane.

You will find a great deal to see most times of the year in the Galapagos. However, there are a few general guidelines to keep in mind. The high seasons for visitation are related to school years and major holidays. This means in most countries the months of December to March and July and August, so book early for these times. In the autumn many of the boats are in dry-dock and the guides are on refresher courses, so there will be fewer boats to choose from at that time.

As for weather, the mildest and driest times generally are October to early December and May to August. Seas are calmer, and days are bright without being unbearably hot on land (on the water, in the moving boat, heat is rarely a problem). March tends to be the hottest month combined with 100-percent humidity. Water temperatures are much cooler from June to September (about 18°C, or 64°F). If you're planning on swimming or snorkeling during this time, bring a wetsuit or check that your boat provides one.

A NOTE ABOUT SAFETY

Safety is an important concern in all outdoor activities. No guidebook can alert you to every hazard or anticipate the limitations of every reader. Therefore, the descriptions of roads, trails, routes, and natural features in this book are not representations that a particular place or excursion will be safe for you or your party. When you follow any of the routes or undertake any activities described in this book, you assume responsibility for your own safety. Under normal conditions, such excursions require the usual attention to traffic, road and trail conditions, the stability and conditions of waterways, weather, terrain, the capabilities of your party, and other factors. Keeping informed on current conditions and exercising common sense are the keys to a safe, enjoyable outing.

—*Mountaineers Books*

4

VISITING THE ISLANDS

. . . .

Travel to the Galapagos Islands has become both simpler and more complex over the years. At one time you booked a boat through a local or Ecuadorean agency, and you lived on that boat for eight days and seven nights. Boats tended to be small, holding between eight and a dozen people, and you had an up-close, personal relationship with the land, water, crew, and other visitors. The route was carefully worked out, but sometimes there was room to take a side trip that passengers found interesting (if the port authority granted your group permission).

These days there are many options for travel. Visitors can both depart from two airports on the mainland and arrive at two airports on the islands. Their schedules will affect your timing and your route—in the Galapagos and back on the mainland, where you will want to spend some time. Visits on the islands can be as short as three or four days, and you can

mix and match time on a boat or on land. Understanding these dramatic changes in travel options will allow you to make an informed choice about your travel mode, timing, and destinations.

TRAVEL MODES—LIVE-ABOARD, ISLAND-HOPPING, DAY TRIPS

There are three main ways to visit the islands: weeklong or shorter "live-aboard" cruises; "island-hopping," combining boat and land stays; and "day tripping," by boat from one of the main island communities—Puerto Ayora, on Santa Cruz, or Puerto Baquerizo Moreno, on San Cristóbal. This variety of options is a fairly recent development, so if you are discussing the trip with friends who traveled to the Galapagos before 2012 or so, they are most likely to have been on the weeklong cruises. This means that while they can share their experiences for that length of trip, living exclusively on a boat, you will want to learn more about the evolving visitation options when making your decision for a trip.

Traveling to the Galapagos has been revolutionized by the internet and by the diversification of visiting options, especially the increased involvement of local residents in hosting tourists. Whatever your visiting mode, you can go directly to the internet to get detailed information about the islands, sites to visit, and the multitude of touring options and tour operators. The key websites to start your planning are:

- Galapagos National Park, www.galapagospark.org, www.galapagos.gob.ec
- Charles Darwin Foundation, www.darwinfoundation.org, especially the DataZone section
- Galapagos Conservancy, www.galapagos.org
- International Galapagos Tour Operators Association, www.igtoa.org

Of course, you'll find a huge array of websites for touring companies around the world that provide travel to the Galapagos and mainland Ecuador. Some touring websites give feedback from travelers and these comments can be very informative, though all of these sources must be read through a comparative, critical lens.

The travel business is "layered," with international tour companies engaging the Galapagos-based services to provide the actual services for your visit. It is important when considering a trip through a non-Galapagos-based travel company (whether in mainland Ecuador or international) to discuss directly with their staff about how closely they work with Galapagos partners, how often their own company staff visit the islands, how up-to-date they are on any changes in visitation rules and regulations, the quality of the boats, and how informed they are about any related land-based services or accommodations provided. Reputable companies have a staff member visiting the islands at least a couple of times a year, often accompanying one of their groups.

Because you can use the internet these days to research services, you can be your own travel agent and contact the tourism operators in the islands directly to book what you want. This approach eliminates a layer of service cost; however, if you should experience difficulties in bookings or quality of facilities or service, they may be difficult to resolve if the company is small. This is particularly true for services located only on the islands as well—whether it be a day-trip provider, a local bed-and-breakfast, or any of the other services of whatever scale of comfort or luxury. The internet can be a help here, but again, caution and comparison are called for.

Live-Aboard Travel

Until fairly recently, the typical mode of visitation was booking an eight-day, seven-night tour, living on the boat (which

Taking in the sight of Kicker Rock, near San Cristóbal

means that you can sleep through the night for most of the inter-island maneuvering). During the day you will be hopping into a *panga*, a small outboard motorboat or inflatable craft, holding ten or twelve passengers and your guide, and taking excursions to different visitor sites. Larger boats will have several pangas to deliver you to the destination and more guides. Typically your first trip of the day will start after breakfast, then you go back on board for lunch and a siesta, followed by an afternoon landing and trail walk. There have been changes in this option, however. Now it is possible to book three-, four-, or five-day live-aboard experiences, which people may combine with staying a

few days in one of the island communities and doing day trips from there.

In my most recent trip, in a boat holding sixteen of us, after several days nearly half of the travelers disembarked and headed to their home countries, to be replaced by another group of the same number. (This second group had already spent some time in Puerto Ayora and environs.) It all went smoothly for everyone, with the usual exchanges of emails, promises to write, and taking of farewell pictures.

There are five levels of boat, and as you do your web search, you will find the following terminology generally used. All boats must have a licensed naturalist guide for every sixteen passengers.

1. **Luxury-Class**
   This type of boat may have facilities such as an onboard swimming pool, a gift shop, or a hot tub. These boats can carry up to one hundred passengers. There are usually two deck levels, relatively spacious cabins, hot- and cold-water showers, and air-conditioning.

2. **First-Class**
   These spacious ships have very comfortable amenities, but they do not have facilities like swimming pools or gift shops. They carry between eighteen and forty-five passengers and have hot and cold water and air-conditioning.

3. **Tourist or Superior-Class**
   These are the most numerous boats, holding from eight to twenty passengers.

They have both ocean-view-level cabins and ones below deck. Cabins are smaller, but comfortable, and there is hot water and air-conditioning.

4. **Tourist-Class**

These boats, hosting around eight to sixteen passengers, have either shared or private bathrooms, and they may have hot water or air-conditioning.

5. **Economy-Class**

The least expensive of the boat options have limited privacy, no air conditioning, and probably no hot water.

There are also sailboats and motorboats, which tend to be in the second and third levels above.

For scuba enthusiasts, because the Galapagos offer such a spectacular diving experience, there are a few authorized boats that specialize in diving in the seventy-five marine sites (though some of these are most suitable for snorkeling only). All of these sites are reached by boat exclusively. A web search will lead to these boats and services. Divers must have the appropriate international training and safety certifications. Because the water is usually very cold and there are challenging currents and locations, intermediate to advanced divers are most likely to be comfortable diving in the islands.

Of course, the cost of the live-aboard depends greatly on the level of boat

Colorful Puerto Baquerizo Moreno, San Cristóbal

chosen. It also varies by whether you are booking directly with the boat company, or by the fee structure of the travel company or the organization that you may be traveling with (fund-raising trips sponsored by conservation groups are common). Because of the changing nature of options, and changes over time, it isn't possible to give prices here. But comparison-shopping via the internet will tell you what you need to know.

The most important thing to find out is the itinerary of the boat. From reading this book and by searching the Galapagos National Park, Galapagos Conservancy, and IGTOA sites you will know which islands have which kinds of land and marine wildlife, plants, geology, human history, interpretive centers, and communities, and you can compare your list with the itinerary of the boat.

I have had the experience of travelers expecting to see a certain kind of bird, limited to one or two sites on a far-flung island—and this was not on our itinerary. The travelers were still delighted with all they'd seen, but it did alert me to the importance of checking your itinerary beforehand. Itineraries can change, even day to day, if weather calls for a route change, or if a volcano makes travel nearby risky, or if the Park Service notes that there are emerging risks for conservation of any aspect of a given visitor site. However, the Park Service sets the itineraries allowed for boats, so you can usually depend on where you will be going on the boat you choose.

With all this discussion of prices and cabins and planning, it may sound as if the whole adventure can be predicted or that if you figure out some exact calculation of cost and space you'll know exactly what will happen. However, the Galapagos is one of those travel destinations where the quality of the experience is not predicated largely on cost. Humans, animals, machines, weather, seasons, and just plain luck all work together to shape your trip.

Island-Hopping

By island-hopping you can spend a few days in several communities, stopping along the way at various visitor sites reached by small boat. This takes some planning, and is probably best arranged by a travel company. They should be able to match up your interests and schedule and budget with a good itinerary for this type of travel. If you plan and make reservations on your own, check to see whether your transfers from the airport to your accommodation and back home are part of the services. Also be sure to find out whether you will be able to follow up on hikes, horseback riding, birding, or other guided activities.

Typically, people will spend a couple of days each in the Puerto Ayora area on Santa Cruz, Puerto Villamil on Isabela Island, and/or Puerto Baquerizo Moreno on San Cristóbal. They'll then do day trips on the local island or to nearby visitor sites. If these are Park Service sites, you will need to have a licensed guide and travel with an authorized day tour provider. You won't cover as much ground or sea this way, or experience being away from the towns in the uninhabited islands, but you may have a better acquaintance with the areas you do spend time in than you might have in the more extensive live-aboard tour option.

While island-hopping can provide a bit more of an in-depth experience of a given island or two, it does limit the breadth of your visiting the Galapagos. You will go to fewer places, so you will see less of the diversity of the geography, of plant life, and of human history. This option is also not necessarily less expensive than one of the mid-level or economy live-aboard tours. As of this writing, a stay in an island hotel, plus food, tours, etc., can be nearly the equivalent daily cost of a five- to full eight-day live-aboard tour, depending again on the class category of the boat.

Day Trips

To be frank, day-tripping is the least desirable travel mode, in my view. Those choosing this option assume it will allow them more freedom of movement (not having to have a guide, etc.) or be cheaper than a fixed cruise option. Day-tripping visitors tend to fly on their own to Baltra or San Cristóbal and stay in Puerto Ayora or Puerto Baquerizo Moreno, perhaps moving between the two after a few days. These communities do have a range of accommo-

dations, including an increasing number of bed-and-breakfast facilities. There are also a number of little shops that offer day tours to nearby islands.

However, at the time of this writing, it must be noted that in these very informal situations quality of accommodations and services can be uneven, and the visitor has little recourse if conditions are poor and activities do not meet expectations. Also because so much of the land and marine base of the Galapagos is within national park boundaries with carefully developed visitation rules, including being with a licensed guide in most locations and for most activities, day-trippers will not have nearly as many opportunities to see a wide range of sites and engage in many activities. There are efforts to develop a rating system for these accommodations and services, but at this point day-tripping is my least-recommended travel option for a Galapagos visit.

DINING AND SHOPPING

Food is always an important part of your trip. On the boats, even the smaller, more modestly priced ones, you are likely to find the food to be fresh, well-prepared, and plentiful. There is an emphasis on a mix of fish, fresh fruits and vegetables, and delicious desserts. The food may be shipped in, but there is an increasing use of agricultural products from the farming areas of the islands. This is part of the efforts to include locals in the benefits of tourism. On the large cruise ships the cuisine and its presentation are at the upper levels of international travel. Meals may be less elaborate on smaller ships, but I have always found them to be attractive, tasty, and filling.

Alcoholic beverages will be available, usually at an added cost to the trip fare, but the plentiful juices, tea, coffee, and treated water will be free. (Bottled water is the usual option throughout the islands and on the boats.) The ship's kitchen will accommodate dietary restrictions, such as food allergies or vegetarianism and even veganism. Usually the agency arranging your trip, whether from abroad or on the islands, will ask you to fill out a form indicating preferences or requirements (this may not be so for day-tripping options).

If you spend a day or two in Puerto Ayora or Puerto Baquerizo Moreno, you will be going on your own or with some of your group to local restaurants or cafes. Just check the menu before you go in. You are likely to have a good choice of chicken, fish, beef, and fresh vegetables, and a good dessert, in a range of prices and serving styles. Your guide will be able to tell you about favorite places and food choices. All of the cafes in these communities are well within walking distance of each other and of the dock where you will have anchored.

In any of the communities you visit, you will be able to top up with any personal items you need. There will be places to get fresh batteries, personal care items, sun hats, another jacket, and sunscreen.

And there are little booths (*cabinas*) where you can make inexpensive international calls and be connected to the internet. The larger boats may have internet as well; be sure to inquire about that before you book your ship. There is a vast array of shops stuffed with every kind of souvenir. Some are the usual T-shirts and caps, but increasingly there are high-style articles of clothing and local crafts, as well as those from the mainland. You'll find plenty of the latter in the markets of the highlands of Ecuador in particular, including traditional crafts and artwork, very striking weaving, and colorful woven clothing of all sorts.

PHYSICAL AND MENTAL REQUIREMENTS

In physical terms, the person who is basically healthy and can scamper up and down a ladder on the side of a heaving boat, get in and out of a lunging launch or *panga* (usually an inflatable Zodiac) at the shore, walk a couple of hours now and then in blazing sun, and withstand a chilly breeze and the slap of a wave across the face will be very happy on the trip.

I suggest that you be able to swim and generally be at ease around water. You won't have to swim, but it is an appealing option. The main thing is that you want to be comfortable in a marine environment. Even if it is new to you, you'll soon get used to the adventure and find it interesting and even thrilling to be a part of it all. In practical terms, the crew will start out with an orientation to safety measures

Sharing the trip of a lifetime, Genovesa

on board, and you'll be required to wear a life jacket on the short trips in the panga that ferries you between the shore and your boat. You'll laugh at yourself and all your puffy companions, and probably take a lot of pictures as you skim along.

Tips for Traveling with Children and Young Adults

For young people, a trip to the Galapagos can be one of the most exciting and educational adventures of their lives. In my experience, young travelers should be at least fourteen years of age to be comfortable with the demands of living on a boat,

sticking to a schedule, eating different foods, and getting along with the same small group for a week or more.

I strongly suggest that they be good swimmers, as they probably will very much want to join in the snorkeling. Because the water is usually quite cold, having a wetsuit is advisable. The ships aren't likely to have wetsuits for sub-adult sizes. Parents should be good swimmers also, as they will be responsible for their children, staying close to them in the water at all times.

Most importantly, to visit the islands, children and young adults must be mature enough to understand that the Galapagos Islands are a natural treasure. That means behavior that might be tolerated elsewhere (such as running off in a different direction, or not paying attention to directions from the naturalist guide) cannot be tolerated here and can be dangerous on cliffs and in other hazardous areas. But many young people are very aware of the importance of protecting our environment, and they have probably seen films on the Galapagos. They would be very happy playing their part in conserving the islands that until the trip they have only seen on a screen or a page.

A child who has a highly developed sense of curiosity, is fairly patient with long boat rides where there may be "nothing to do" except sit or read or draw, and can put up with sunburn or seasickness and unfamiliar food, will enjoy this trip.

Accessibility for Those with Mobility Impairments

For my latest trip, I made an informal assessment of accessibility of travel in the islands for a friend who has mobility impairments. My reference was a person with a neurological condition who is able to walk with canes for short distances and can walk longer with a wheeled "walker." The person also uses an electric scooter, which could be transported by air. In the towns and on the boat and on the trails, I tried to assess what would be doable for this person for a visit to the Galapagos.

In the towns the roads are often rough, with ruts or potholes or cobbled surfaces. This is so for all but the main sections of the main streets of each community. Walking with aids, or arm in arm with a friend, would be possible, though not easy. I did see a person being wheeled in a chair in Puerto Ayora, but this would work only on the main road, which is fairly smooth and level. An additional impediment to access in the towns is that almost all streets have high sidewalks and the shops or cafes are set on another layer of steps, high ones. There are not curb cuts, and the secondary streets are gravel or dirt.

In contrast, the latest Park Service buildings are often wheelchair accessible, but getting there is the problem. The highest-end hotels may have ramps, but in visiting one of the main hotels in Puerto Ayora I found the ramps so steep and so short that any motorized scooter would simply have gotten stuck at the transition to the floor itself.

There are a number of taxis in the communities, but these are light half-trucks, and while the drivers would no doubt be very helpful, there are no lower steps or adapted seats, and the walker or scooter would have to be hauled into the back.

For being on the boat, the most likely accommodation would be on the very high-end cruise ships. They have elevators from floor to floor and enough room in the salons and decks to get around with mobility aids. Their programming is set at three levels of "intensity," because their clientele includes persons whose health and stamina may be somewhat limited. Thus, for a given visitor site one intensity level may be a ride in the panga around the area of interest, seeing the marine life or birds on the cliffs from that vantage point. An intermediate level for the same site may be walking with one of the guides on the shorter loop of a trail. The most intense level may be going with another group for the full circuit of the island trail. There is no option for wheelchairs on the trails. A visitor must be able to walk.

The nature of the trails varies considerably. Some trails are wide, firm, and fairly level. However, many are rocky, slippery, narrow, and intermittently steep. If you are on a mid-sized to smaller boat, with some sixteen passengers and one guide attending to the entire group, there is not the option of offering various intensities of visit. It could be that one of the crew can take you in a ride in the panga around a cove or along a point of land while the others walk the trail, but they cannot leave the area because they must be ready to help with the ship and would not have permission to deviate from the ship's itinerary.

In such cases the large cruise ships would be the sole source to be explored further, keeping in mind that even then many of the visitor sites would not be accessible for those requiring adaptive equipment. If a visitor travels with a companion who stabilizes them, this may work in some situations, but it has to be kept in mind that in a number of places, the trail is narrow, and only single-file walking is possible.

5

TRAVEL ESSENTIALS

....

This section assumes a trip that is largely live-aboard, for a full week. You should be able to adapt this to a somewhat different itinerary and travel mode.

CLOTHING

The clothing you bring for the Galapagos will in many cases be useful if you spend time on the mainland of Ecuador—whether in the cities and countryside of the Andes, the rain forest, or in the lowlands along the coast. The main difference would be in having a set of warmer clothes and heavier shoes for the Andes section, as detailed in the "Weather and Clothing" section of chapter 16. For your Galapagos visit, be sure to have the following items, with as many of them as possible hand-washable and easy to dry:

- 2 pairs long pants, lightweight (zip-off legs are great)
- 1 pair sturdy, lightweight shorts
- 1 bathing suit
- 1 wetsuit if snorkeling, full dry or wet suit if scuba diving
- One-week supply of underwear
- 1 or 2 tank tops
- 1 or 2 short-sleeved shirts
- 2 long-sleeved, long-body lightweight shirts
- 1 hooded sweatshirt
- 1 windbreaker or lightweight rain jacket
- 1 pair of waterproof or amphibious sandals that have rugged soles with good traction, and closed toe areas to protect against rocks and spiky brush
- 1 pair sturdy running shoes or lightweight hiking boots
- One-week supply of socks
- 1 large floppy hat with a chin strap

TOILETRIES, MEDICINES, AND OTHER PERSONAL EFFECTS

Even though you can replace many articles that you may lose or run out of, be sure to bring your own toiletries, medicines, and other personal items.

• Towel (boat and accommodations provide towels, but bring one along if you have a favorite)
• Sunblock (as strong as possible)
• Sunglasses (and strap to hold them on in the wind)
• Flashlight (for lava-tube visits or night-time walking about in mainland haciendas or rain-forest lodges)
• Mosquito and bug repellent
• Small sewing kit
• Eyeglasses, including sunglasses or eye-shades
• Prescription and other medications
• Anti-seasickness medications

To elaborate on a couple of items: Take two pairs of glasses, and observe the same precautions as you would for medications. An eyeglass repair kit can turn out to be invaluable. Your best bet is to keep medicines with you in your carry-on bag on planes and until you settle in to your boat or other accommodation. And for extra precaution, carry two sets, each kept in a separate place.

If you are taking pills for seasickness, start taking them a couple of days before you sail. Once on board, take one pill every four hours during the day and at bedtime for the next two or three days. In my experience, if you build up the medication in your system early on, you should be able to avoid discomfort. If you forget

to bring pills with you, any pharmacy in Quito or Guayaquil will have the local equivalent. Just say "Galapagos" and look queasy, and they will get the picture. As for the various metal bracelets, pressure-point bandages, etc., the best advice I can give is to check with a knowledgeable healthcare provider, test it yourself if you can, check with friends, and just do what seems best.

EQUIPMENT AND FIELD GUIDES

What equipment you bring reflects your own interests. The most important would be binoculars and cameras and lens cleaner for these. It's important to have a watertight sack for when you are going back and forth on the panga for the excursions. All of these can go in a small day pack, along with an unbreakable water flask, which you can fill from the boat's supply before each excursion. Be sure to bring extra batteries and any of the chargers that come with your electronic equipment. Ecuador and the islands are on 110 volts, and most plugins are compatible.

For your Galapagos trip as a whole, you should bring a Galapagos guidebook, and if you are a birder or snorkeler, bring a field guide for birds or marine life. There are many sources for these right in Puerto Ayora, including the excellent gift shop of the Galapagos National Park. You can get many of the books before you leave, but if you're shopping along the way, the Libri Mundi bookstores, found in Quito,

Flightless cormorant drying its minimal wings in the wind, Fernandina

Guayaquil, and most larger communities on the mainland, are well supplied with a very wide variety of books, maps, and writing materials for diarists. If you don't have a copy of Darwin's *Voyage of the Beagle*, consider getting one. It is delightful reading; he has a wry sense of humor, and it's like walking along with him around the world. Better yet, the Galapagos chapter is still relevant. There are also a number of outfitting stores, both in Puerto Ayora and Puerto Baquerizo Moreno, which stock local and international brands of clothing and other adventure equipment.

Cameras and Photography

Many people carry video equipment, but this is mostly small and hand-held. Most digital cameras have sufficient capacity for high-quality filming to show to folks back home or to upload to the internet.

Just remember that you will be getting on and off boats several times a day, so insure everything before you go and don't take anything you're not prepared to watch sink to the bottom of the ocean. Also consider an underwater camera. You may be using one only for this trip, but there are inexpensive waterproof point-and-shoot cameras that do very well indeed for the snorkeler or person who is just wading along the shore and wants to dip the camera in to take a picture of submerged creatures like sea stars or even a swimming marine iguana.

Photographic equipment has changed so drastically over the last few years that my advice is quite simple. First of all, be sure you know how to use your camera before you go. I've often seen people buy a brand-new camera for the trip, and then spend many frustrating hours trying to

Shelf fungi in the moist highlands of Santa Cruz

zoom is optical, not digital, and that your camera has high definition. This is very important for being able to enlarge pictures and retain sharpness. Some people do have the more elaborate outfits, with SLR bodies and various lenses. That is a matter of personal preference and the use you will have for your pictures when you get home.

It is a good idea to carry two cameras, in case you drop one overboard. Taking one of the more elaborate point-and-shoot formats and then one of the larger SLR formats will give you the insurance you need. Few of the point-and-shoot cameras have a polarizing attachment capacity, however.

For your whole trip, if you are visiting the mainland, then consider when choosing equipment that birdlife will be farther away, especially in the highlands or rain forest. Telephoto is called for, but again, today's digital cameras have a huge zoom capacity, and the camera can still be light and easily maneuverable. A good macro capacity is also important, for taking pictures of insects, fungi, flowers. All of the cameras have this, but do make sure you know how to use it.

Both in the Galapagos or on the mainland, because you will be taking so many pictures, use a high-capacity memory card in your cameras. I use a 16- or 32-gigabyte card in both cameras, but also download daily to my laptop (and to a separate USB drive on a daily basis, which is kept separate from everything else as a further

figure out all the dials and buttons on it. Above all, you'll need a polarizing filter, especially for the Galapagos, with its marine environment. If you include mainland Ecuador in your travels, you will be glad to have a polarizing filter option for the rain forest and for the many lakes and rivers in the highlands.

As for whether you will want to bring a telephoto lens, in the Galapagos the wildlife is generally very near, so a focal length of 300 millimeters or so is sufficient. Even most point-and-shoot cameras have at least this capacity. Just make sure your

security measure). Of course, you can have a much higher-capacity memory card in your camera and rely entirely on that, but things do go wrong. A dropped camera, some electronic glitch, and there go your photographic memories of your trip.

Also, if you do transfer all the pictures from the memory card to another location, reformat the empty card before you use it again. It's usually an option on the camera menu.

Diving and Snorkeling

Most boats supply snorkeling equipment, and unless you are an unusual size or particularly fastidious, this should be sufficient. If you are visiting the islands between June and September, when the water is coolest, think about bringing a wetsuit for snorkeling (or check that your boat provides one) if you want to do more than leap in and out for a quick glimpse below the surface. If you are scuba diving, you will want a full wet or dry suit for your comfort and safety.

Scuba diving is a growing activity in the islands, but you must book with a boat that specializes in this and has the appropriate support systems, including the capacity to refill air tanks. The Park Service requires that the boat have a special naturalist guide who is also licensed as a diver. The boat must book an itinerary that concentrates on the diving sites, some of which are different from the sites for dry-landers. Some operators will

Snorkeling at Devil's Crown

Jeroen Nijenstein and Eva Mulder

arrange for dive opportunities using the local land-based dive shops. Bring your diving certifications.

PASSPORT AND OTHER DOCUMENTATION

All international visitors must have a current passport. This is true for visiting the Galapagos and entering Ecuador. The entry document given to visitors must be presented upon leaving Galapagos, so do put it with your passport for safekeeping. Boats vary as to whether the passport remains with the traveler or is kept in the boat's safe for the trip.

As with any international travel, it's a good idea to make three photocopies of your passport and your tickets before you leave home. Leave one with your travel agent or with a friend or colleague who can be easily reached if something happens to the original. Carry the originals with you and put the other set of copies in a separate place in your luggage. If you lose your passport or tickets, it will be easier to overcome this problem if you have these photocopies as a record.

CURRENCY AND FEES

Ecuador uses the US dollar as the national currency, so any conversion you do from your home currency will be on that basis. You simply use US dollars everywhere, in the Galapagos and mainland Ecuador. You will find prices are generally lower than US or European equivalents for items you buy. Many places do not accept $50 or $100 US bills, so take smaller bills with you.

There is a 12-percent value-added tax for all transactions in Ecuador and a 10-percent charge for services. Also there usually is an additional 10-percent charge for credit card purchases. Be sure to determine whether any fees cited in advertisements for travel or accommodations include the value-added and service charges. Some options may seem less expensive than others but in reality are not, once the taxes are taken into account.

You will pay for cold drinks and beer on the boat, aside from the cost for the trip itself. I suggest allocating about 10 percent of the cost of your boat tour for tips for the naturalist and crew. The tips usually are put into a kitty and given to the captain to distribute. Crew wages are usually low, and the tips are most welcome. You don't have to tip, but you probably will want to thank the crew and naturalist guide in this way. Chances are you will be extremely impressed and even touched by the expert and solicitous care you receive from the captain and crew.

The current Galapagos National Park fee is $100 per adult and $50 for children under twelve. Your tour operator may include this in your costs and forward this for you. If you are traveling independently, just have the money ready. Your tour operator certainly should be able to update you on any changes in this and make sure you are carrying the right kind and amount of cash for your various

Dazzlingly white beach at Gardner Bay

fees. There is also a $10 fee for park entry referred to as a transit control card. It is a general service fee for supporting control of migration from the mainland, so that movement in and out of the islands by tourists and residents can be kept track of. Have it ready in cash when you enter.

When you are in transit, and in virtually all mainland cities of Ecuador before you arrive in the Galapagos, you can get cash at automated transfer machines, assuming you have connections with the standard international transfer services. It is a good idea to bring some cash in small denominations with you. There are ATM machines in Puerto Ayora and Puerto Baquerizo Moreno, but internet access is not always fully functional. Do be sure to tell your financial institution before you leave that you are going abroad, so that your accounts will not be blocked. You can pay for services, meals, souvenirs, or other items by credit card just about everywhere on the mainland and at a few of the high-end restaurants and stores in the Galapagos, though most small-scale vendors take only cash in the islands and in mainland markets.

COMMUNICATIONS

You'll find access to the internet and email connections in little shops (cabinas) in Puerto Ayora on Santa Cruz and in Puerto Baquerizo Moreno on San Cristóbal. The larger boats tend to have internet connections, but there are additional fees and they can be rather high. Internet can be slow and transfers of large amounts of data can be problematic, because the islands rely on satellite connections. But it does work overall.

When I first went to the islands, phone connections were risky at best and fax or other communications were very modest. Now international phoning is easy. You can go to any of the *cabinas* in these two towns in the Galapagos and throughout mainland Ecuador. In the cabinas, often part of cafes or sometimes stand-alone, you can make international calls at just pennies a minute. I have found the assistants to be very helpful, so don't worry if you speak little or no Spanish. Cell phones generally work, but be sure to check with your provider about long-distance usage fees. You can buy local use cards in most communities of any size.

Opposite: *Olive-sand beach, Floreana*

PART III

MAJOR ISLANDS AND
VISITOR SITES IN
THE GALAPAGOS

There are now seventy terrestrial visitor sites and seventy-five marine visitor sites in the Galapagos National Park, quite an increase from my first visit in 1981! Since then the most dramatic change has been the addition of the marine visitor sites, the snorkeling and diving sites, established when the Marine Reserve became a part of the park. This guidebook focuses on the land sites, many of which I have visited during my ten trips over the years.

I snorkel readily but I am not a diver, and while diving is extremely popular in the islands, it's best if someone in the diving world provides you with detailed information on these sites. An excellent start for learning about these sites is the Galapagos National Park website, www.galapagospark.org. Many of the diving sites are adjacent to the land sites—for example, at Plaza Sur, Seymour Norte, and Devil's Crown. Visitors will walk along the trails, but may also snorkel at the beaches, all listed on the park website under terrestrial and marine sites.

In this section the land sites that you are most likely to visit are described, along with any water activities at adjacent marine sites. In a very few cases I have had to rely on the excellent descriptions on the Park Service website, supplemented by talking with local experts, guides, and other visitors. But for the most part what follows is my own personal guide to the sites, my own sense of the experience of being there. Think of this as walking along with me as we visit the truly enchanted islands of the Galapagos.

Baltra is not an official visitor site where you will be greeted by one of the licensed naturalist guides and told about its very special flora and fauna. But Baltra's Aeropuerto Seymour, the "first Ecological Airport," is one of the two principal airports, and so it may be your first landing site. Even as your flight approaches the islands, you will be learning about their distinctive nature, just by observing the weather.

If you are there from June through December, which is the *garua* season, it is likely that there will be masses of low-level clouds. These skies protect you to some degree from the sun, but the glare can make photography difficult. During these months there is often misty rain, but the clouds foretell a chill to the air at times, particularly in the evenings.

As the islands show through the clouds, the land looks mostly coppery-brown and gray. Conical landforms predominate, from hillocks to mountains. The large number and various sizes of the islands usually come as a surprise to visitors. The shorelines gleam white, and the near-shore water is the turquoise blue so often associated with tropical islands. The final approach takes you over Mosquera Island, a brilliant white sand spit that you may be able to visit later.

Even as you walk from the plane to the recently built eco-friendly airport building on Baltra, you may see land iguanas in the nearby brush. Since feral cats were eradicated from the island in 2005, the iguanas have made a definite comeback.

As you leave the building, take some time to look a little farther to the scrub areas nearby. You are sure to see the first Darwin's finches of the trip scrabbling around on the ground. A couple of different beak sizes will be evident, and so will be the browns of the females and the blacks of the males. There won't be time here for much more than a glance, but when (after a short bus ride) you embark on a boat you have booked for a tour, or the short ferry ride to Puerto Ayora on Santa Cruz, if you are continuing your travels from there. Either way you will already be seeing another well-known Galapagos inhabitant—sea lions along the water's edge, or diving around the boats.

If you are going directly to a boat for a multiday tour, this would be the time to take your seasick pills (although it is best to have started the morning before leaving the mainland and then take another one on the boat). Then just go out on the deck and start absorbing the ambience of these exotic islands. There also should be a safety briefing at this time, and the guide will tell you about the park rules for behaving appropriately, in a careful manner, throughout the park.

As the boat moves out into the open sea, you may see blue-footed boobies busily diving for fish or standing basking on rocks. The first sight of a booby's wheeling plunge into the aquamarine sea seems to signal that your island adventure has really begun. Pelicans may join the boobies in their hunt, and lava gulls often come to sit on the *panga* (or inflatable Zodiac) that is tied to the larger boat. A sea lion may even hop up into the boat's fantail or up on the panga. Everyone will call everyone else over to come and look, but the sea lion generally is oblivious to the attention.

6

SANTA CRUZ

Santa Cruz, the second largest of the islands, is located near the center of the Galapagos archipelago. It is volcanic in origin, and rises from sea level to a gentle cone. Its highlands rise to a height of 864 meters (2835 feet). Because of its altitude changes, there is a variety of habitat, which creates a number of different plant and wildlife viewing opportunities. Santa Cruz has a population of approximately eighteen thousand, with the major concentration being in the main community and central port of Puerto Ayora. It is also very likely that you will spend at least a day in Puerto Ayora, with visits to the highlands to see tortoises rambling in their natural habitat.

Puerto Ayora is the town most geared toward tourism, with a wide range of hotels, restaurants, day excursion options, and shopping. It is centrally located in the archipelago as a whole, has many visitor sites, and is the home of the Charles Darwin Research Station, the Tortoise Breeding Center, and the headquarters of the Galapagos National Park Directorate ("Park Service" from now on in these descriptions).

PLAYA LAS BACHAS

This brilliantly white beach with its plant-lined dune and small lagoon is a destination on the northern side of Santa Cruz and often the first stop for all boats that have taken on passengers from the Baltra airport. The ride is only an hour or so away, so Playa las Bachas is reached in mid- to late afternoon. It is a wet landing, where the panga pulls into shallow water or right up on shore and then everyone hops out. It's best to carry your lightweight walking shoes and disembark barefoot. The beach is sandy, and because the cove is sheltered, the water is rarely rough, so it's an easy landing.

Las Bachas is an immersion into one of the most typical Galapagos shoreline environments. First, there is the white

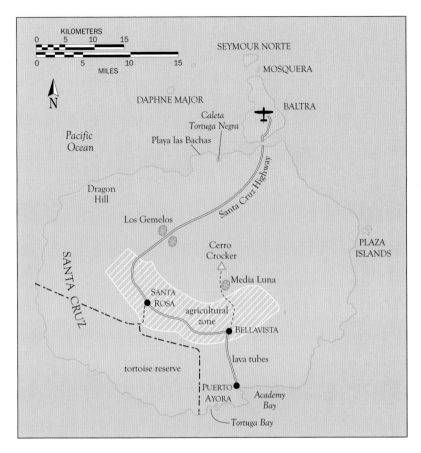

sand beach, in contrast to beaches on some of the other islands which may have red or black sand, depending on the local rock composition. This beach is a major egg-laying site for sea turtles. You can see indentations in the sand, and among the beach plants higher up from the beach, where sea turtles lay their eggs. You may spot trails left by the adults or departing hatchlings as they make their way to the sea. Your guide will point out where you may safely walk and what areas to avoid.

Where the beach rises to a low crest, there is a band of tangled saltbush (*Cryptocarpus pyriformis*) with some prickly pear cactus (*Opuntia helleri*). Next you approach a small lagoon, of brackish water. Here you'll have a good chance of seeing a couple of shorebird species, the common stilt, (*Himantopus mexicanus*) or

Herd of Sally Lightfoot crabs, Santa Cruz

wandering tattler (*Heteroscelus incanum*) and with luck there may be a few flamingos (*Phoenicopterus ruber*). They sieve plankton and tiny crustaceans as they wander along, leaving trails in the algae on the surface of the lagoon and in the mud at the bottom.

Along the shore and in the bushes, you will almost certainly see your first marine iguanas. They sit quietly, occasionally doing push-ups in place. It's easy to take pictures, although you should take care to compensate for the blackness of the iguana's skin in comparison with the glaring white sand.

In this area I took one of my favorite marine iguana pictures, very close up. It was a real Galapagos experience, in that by framing it just right I was able to disguise the fact that it was a crowded scene. Six other people ringed the iguana, and four different languages were being spoken—quietly but excitedly—as we all snapped away. The iguana seemed to be oblivious.

On your return to the beach area, some of the group may want to do a little snorkeling; this is a nice, quiet place to learn to breathe, use flippers, and observe marine life—all at once. The guide will have planned for this, if there is time, and you can use your own snorkeling equipment or pick from the boat's supply. For this short a swim, in shallow water, you won't want to bother with struggling into a wetsuit.

Your return to the panga will mark the first time for an important Galapagos ritual: foot cleaning. It is imperative that you wash off any sand, seeds, or other

Flamingos between the beach and a lagoon, Santa Cruz

debris from your feet and shoes. This is to prevent the artificial transport of plant life or bacteria from one island to another and to help keep the boat clean. The crew helps by using hoses to wash you off.

PUERTO AYORA

Puerto Ayora is the largest of the four communities on the islands. Most tours bring their clients for at least half a day there, and it is also a frequent destination (or starting point) for island-hopping or day-tripping. Puerto Ayora is of particular interest to the conservation-oriented visitor, because both the Charles Darwin Research Station and the headquarters of the Galapagos National Park Directorate (Park Service) are located there. It is also the home of the largest and oldest Tortoise Breeding Center (see below).

Puerto Ayora is also a supply center for the boats, which come in here between trips to replenish supplies.

Puerto Ayora is the most developed community in the islands in terms of amenities for the visitor. You can stay overnight in accommodations ranging from a basic bed-and-breakfast, to a modest hotel, to a very high-end hotel with ocean views. You can eat in a growing variety of restaurants serving everything from traditional Ecuadorean fare to sushi, pizza, and nearly haute cuisine dining. The main street and side streets have many shops where you can do your souvenir shopping (from T-shirts and postcards, to locally made art pieces and jewelry). The islands have a large resident group of indigenous peoples from the highlands of mainland Ecuador who sell their woolen goods

Marine iguana sipping water, San Cristóbal

such as sweaters, rugs, and tapestries, often with images of Galapagos plants and animals. You can mail your postcards in town; all mine mailed from here made it to their destinations. Banking and communications are readily available here also.

Puerto Ayora is large enough that it provides all the facilities and services that can be found in the home country of just about all visitors. This includes physician services and a hospital. There is also a hyperbaric chamber. The chamber was established to protect divers, whether locals or visitors.

Because of the changes in how people can visit the Galapagos and the great increase in visitors traveling on their own, or staying in Puerto Ayora for island-hopping or day trips, there is a very wide variety of local tourism operations to match just about any interest. This includes the range of accommodation, options for scuba diving or snorkeling excursions, day trips to nearby visitor sites, or walking and hiking trips to the highlands of Santa Cruz. If you are traveling independently, you can simply walk into any of these offices to ask about what they offer, the prices, the schedules. Comparison-shopping can be rewarding.

If you have time just to walk around town, you can still enjoy the marine life right from the landing pier or along the waterfront. From the dock itself, you can peer down into the water below with a chance of seeing some baby sharks, sea

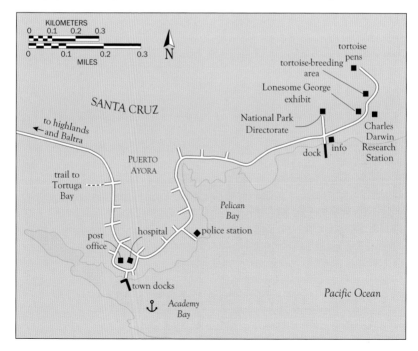

turtles, and colorful fish. There will probably be sea lions diving and rolling in the water and pelicans resting on the pier railings or diving into the water for a meal.

The area at the base of the main pier has been upgraded to a very attractive park that is perfect for just walking, sitting, and observing local life (and other visitors). At the edge of the park is a small stage where musicians may be playing. You might also get to see a game of "ecua-volleyball," an often highly competitive game very different from regular or beach volleyball. It is played throughout Ecuador. The net is very high, with just three players to a side, who catch the ball

and then throw it very high to reach very strategic places that make the return difficult. Spiking is not a key here, deliberate placement is.

You might also take the Gusanito ("little worm"), a delightful little motorized train of colorful cars, each holding four to six people, on a twenty-minute tour around the town. It's well worth the time, a chance to see more than just tourist services in the streets that stretch back from the port and the main road. There are hardware stores, ship chandlers, laundries, schools, churches, motor repair shops, bakeries—a full range of support for this small community.

The Puerto Ayora fish market, Santa Cruz

If you are in town on a Saturday, the local market is not to be missed. It is just a couple of blocks from the main street, sheltered under a large roof, so you're protected rain or shine. It is a wonderful opportunity to spend some time among the local people, who come to shop, eat, catch up with friends, or to buy or sell produce, crafts, or fish. A visit to the market or a stop at the fish market on the main street, not far from the main dock downtown, can give you a bit of a sense of how the local residents of the island carry out their daily lives.

MIGUEL CIFUENTES VISITOR CENTER AND FAUSTO LLERENA TORTOISE BREEDING CENTER

The Miguel Cifuentes Visitor Center is named for the man who was the Superintendent of the Galapagos National Park between 1976 and 1986—a time of great change, as the park took a rapidly increasing role in conservation and sustainability of the islands. Cifuentes played a leadership role not only in Galapagos but on the international conservation stage. It is open to the community as a whole, and is a place for ongoing education and communication within the community and with the outside world—whether tourists, educators, students, or researchers.

The visitor center is an easy 1.8-mile stroll of about an hour from the port's main dock. The Galapagos National Park Directorate and the Charles Darwin Foundation have their headquarters in the same area. It is not an official visitor site, but is visited by most travelers. Take the time to peek at the Park Directorate grounds, along with the office buildings, and you will see an extremely attractive patio area that has a lovely combination of artwork and benches. The paintings of local land and marine life are quite beautiful and a definite addition to the working environment of the Park Service.

As you walk toward the visitor center, the first building along the trail is the Van Straelen Interpretation Center where there are some interpretive exhibits about conservation of the islands and the work of the Park Service and Charles Darwin Research Station.

The Fausto Llerena Tortoise Breeding Center on these grounds is the core of the captive rearing program and tortoise research. The center has both tortoise rearing and observation areas. Rest rooms are here, also. It is important to remember that you are entering an actual restoration project. This is not a zoo, but a work area where visitors are allowed to be close to this crucial work. You'll see a number of enclosures where the young tortoises are being nurtured until they are old enough to be released safely on their home islands.

The results of captive rearing can be spectacular. For example, fourteen surviving adult giant tortoises were removed from Española in the late 1960s because their situation was so precarious. Over the years since then, some two thousand young and sturdy juveniles have been reintroduced to the island. Thanks to their care at the breeding center and the restoration of the Española habitat, these tortoises will live their natural lives on their home island.

For the other tortoise populations, which are still reproducing on their home islands, hatchlings and eggs are collected from the traditional nesting sites, brought in to the breeding center, and placed in protective pens or incubators until they hatch. You will see several different species on display. Others are raised in pens beyond the areas that are not accessible to the public. The very young tortoises you will see are from one to five years old. A typical five-year-old measures about 30 centimeters (12 inches) across. Their carapaces have numbers painted on them to help keep track of each individual while at the center.

After four or five years, a tortoise usually is big enough to survive on its home ground if its natural food supply is sufficient; at this age it is large enough to escape being eaten by rats. Tortoises are tagged before leaving the center so that their progress can be monitored. Some tortoises cannot be returned to their original homes until ways are found to reduce or eradicate the threats to their survival.

The corrals were once home to Lonesome George, the last living example of the Pinta Island tortoise that passed away in 2012. A commemorative sign has been placed at the viewing point of his corral where you can think for a few moments about this grand old man who represented the very last of his race in the entire world.

Geneticists have found some tortoises with partial DNA from Pinta Island. This is good news for the island, because it has no other invasive animals and few invasive plants, so there is the possibility

Commemorating Lonesome George, Santa Cruz

of placing related giant tortoises there for full restoration. The center currently plans to send to Pinta a number of young Española tortoises, genetically the closest cousin to the Pinta species. Modern technology such as traceable tags will help locate them again. Thirty-nine sterilized adult tortoises were released on Pinta in 2009 to measure their impact on vegetation before returning even more tortoises there.

This tortoise visitation area generally is a very busy place, but with all the people there, it is still possible to observe very closely how the tortoises move and feed and even doze with their head resting on an outstretched foot. It is fascinating to watch them chewing away on the paddles of the very aptly named prickly pear cactus. How do they avoid the cactus spines when they chew? Tough gums, our guide explains. My favorite sight there is the yellow warblers darting around the tortoises, drinking their water, snacking on the occasional insect drawn to the tortoises' food. These tiny golden jewels contrast so sharply with the massive, slow-moving tortoises that it is somehow very moving to see them together.

The visitor center grounds have been transformed dramatically over the years to bring the visitor closer to the lowlands habitat in which the station is situated. Wonderful elevated boardwalks snake back into the thick brush, studded with huge *Opuntia* cactus like those you will see on Santa Fe or Plaza Sur. These board-walks make for one of the most beautiful, comfortable, and nonintrusive experi-ences of the lowland habitat. There are shaded patios at several locations along the pathways. Take a few minutes to sit and just enjoy a moment of quiet contem-plation of these surroundings.

The boardwalks also are excellent places for picking out finches, lizards, warblers, bees, and the occasional hawk. You can see up to eight of the Darwin's finches in this area, so keep a look out for the ground finches, the woodpecker finch, or note the long beak of the cactus finch. In some seasons, watch out for the (introduced) wasps; they love sweet things and fresh water and may aim for your lips! The visitor center is already an interest-ing place to visit, but there are plans for a major upgrade soon with new exhibits and trails.

While you're in this area, visit the excellent national park gift shop. It is very attractive, with a variety of styles and products and some items that can be found only there.

The entrance road takes you near the edges of the mangroves that line the shore of the outskirts of Puerto Ayora. Keep a close lookout for lava herons fishing here and there. Lava lizards abound alongside the road, and marine iguanas often are seen in the low-lying mangrove areas near the entrance to the visitor center grounds.

Also near the entrance path, on your right at the edge of the main part of

town, is the local cemetery. All of the graves are aboveground, with edifices of many shapes and sizes for containing the departed. Every year on November 1 and 2, the cemetery's edifices and grounds are renewed for the "Day of the Dead," when the families and friends of the deceased come to clean and refresh the whole area out of respectful memory of their loved ones. The buildings gleam; there are new flowers everywhere, artificial and real. It is a festive yet somber glimpse into the life of the Galapagos people.

THE HIGHLANDS OF SANTA CRUZ

Many of the islands' visitor sites are very near sea level, so there are not many opportunities to experience the moist, lush habitat at the higher elevations. These are the transition, *Scalesia* and *Miconia* zones (described in chapter 2). Santa Cruz is your best opportunity for visiting these zones, because of the range of altitude on this island and the easy access to them. Visit them by bus, taxi, or bicycle if you want the exercise. A cycle path is being constructed between Puerto Ayora and the small towns of Bellavista and Santa Rosa along the main road across the island to the airport.

Most tours include a trip to the high-lands as a regular part of their itinerary. There is a mixture of official national park visitor sites, including the pit cra-ters called Los Gemelos ("the twins"), the crescent-shaped Media Luna, and lava tubes also near the main road. But there are also a number of other lava tubes and pit craters on private property that can be visited for a small fee. Local farmers have diversified their activities to become a part of eco-tourism on the islands. This highlands area and the farms you can visit are anywhere from 30 minutes to more than an hour (by car) from Puerto Ayora. The hikes in the area can last from a few minutes to several hours.

The paths in any of the official or privately protected areas are generally very easy to follow. There are several things to notice along the way. In the *Scalesia* zone you'll see plant life typical of the rich, humid environment. The *Scalesia* trees are much leafier than the spare palo santo

trees seen in the drier, lower areas. Their bark is covered with lichen, and tufts of moss sway in the mild breezes.

Bird-watching is excellent in this area. Sadly the vermilion flycatcher is rarely seen now, but with luck you may get a glimpse of this tiny bird. On my latest visit to one of the farms, we paused at a small pond, and there were several Galapagos pintail ducks and also the Galapagos gallinule. Its shiny bluish-black body contrasted strikingly with the tiny pink algae that coated the pond. Short-eared owls can often be seen in these forested areas as well. And there certainly will be tortoises. In fact, they seem to like the paths as much as humans do, and they

Giant tortoise free-ranging in moist highlands, Santa Cruz

also will be seen as they wander around in the deep grass of the pastures. Vehicles taking the roads into the farms have to slow down from time to time to let a tortoise lumber across the road!

Seeing these beasts is unforgettable. On one trip, as I eagerly looked for them, suddenly there was a tortoise, and then another in a few minutes and only a few meters away. Their backs were a little taller than the bushes, and at first all I could see was the top of the carapace. And as I got closer they made a hissing noise. It turns out this is not a hostile vocalization, but air being expressed, as from a bellows, when they pull in their heads and feet, creating the puffing sound with little whistling overtones. Even when they feed, they puff as they shift their heads, a very soft and pleasant sound.

The chance of sighting tortoises varies somewhat by the season, with encounters more likely in the moister and cooler times (roughly June to December). To ensure your trip is comfortable, bring a light rain jacket or windbreaker, because it can get fairly damp and chilly at these elevations. Lightweight slacks or heavier walking shorts should be adequate, and sturdy shoes that you don't mind getting damp and muddy also are a good idea. Many of the farms provide rubber boots, but it's best to be prepared, just in case they don't have your size or you prefer your own footwear.

These farms also often have small cafes and gift shops, so you'll be able to have a comfortable and dry pause after your walk, sipping the locally grown coffee or having a cold drink, and buying the requisite T-shirt or plush tortoise toy for the kids in your life.

MEDIA LUNA

The trip to Media Luna, named for its halfmoon-shaped volcanic cinder cone, is accessed by car along an easy-to-follow, gently ascending road. Heavy mists are common, so a rain jacket is a definite asset.

To get to Media Luna, you will be driven through the settlement of Bellavista, 7 kilometers (4.3 miles) from Puerto Ayora, and then head toward the high point of the cone. You can walk from Bellavista if you wish, which takes about an hour. First the trail passes through the agricultural zone, and there are avocado and papaya groves, and cattle farms.

As you continue up the gentle slope, the walk enters a mix of Miconia forest, which is found only in a few parts of the Galapagos, and continues into the grassy pampa (fern and sedge) vegetation zone. There is a particularly good opportunity to see the giant ferns there. They tower overhead, and it is almost eerie to look up to a fern and see that its delicate fiddlehead is so large. This area has been under restoration for several years, and the park wardens have eliminated invasive plants such as quinine from more than 30 hectares (75 acres) to reveal a healthy stand of Miconia now in full recovery.

The bird-watching is good, with a likelihood of seeing the woodpecker finch and large tree finches. At the higher levels, the upper limit of the *Miconia* zone, the Galapagos rail (*Laterallus spilonotus*) may be heard and a little lower down lives the equally seldom-seen paint-billed crake (*Neocrex erythrops*). Galapagos petrels (*Pterodroma phaeopygia*) also nest in this area, and the Park Service undertakes regular control of feral animals that can severely hamper the petrels' nesting success. These birds have been designated by the IUCN as *critically endangered*.

On clear days, a visit to Media Luna is very rewarding; the view extends all the way down the sloping side of Santa Cruz to Puerto Ayora and out to nearby islands. This sweep of lush forest, grassland, and the overview of the port community as a whole, with its turquoise harbor of the port, is wonderful, and a striking contrast to the often dry and sparse environs at sea level.

LAVA TUBES

Lava tubes are formed by rushing rivers of lava whose outer surface cooled more quickly than the interior of the flowing mass, hardening sooner. The inner part continued to flow until emptying itself onto the earth or reaching the ocean, thus leaving a hollow tube behind. Tubes vary in size, from a few centimeters to large, complex cavelike structures. There are a number of readily accessible lava tubes on Santa Cruz. Two of them are

official visitor sites, which may be a part of your tour, but the local farmers are also creating opportunities to visit lava tubes on their own property. Your tour guide will know about them, and also in Puerto Ayora there are a number of the tourist agencies that offer excursions to tubes here in the highlands.

There is something fascinating about lava tubes, about being able to walk in the heart of what was a lava flow. The tubes vary in their size, shape, and depth. Some can be entered at ground level; some have ladders for going below. You'll want to have shoes that have a good grip, because the walking can be uneven and often slippery. Also be prepared to have wet feet if the tube is deep enough to collect water. Bring along a flashlight.

LOS GEMELOS

Los Gemelos ("the twins") are two pit craters: sections of the earth's surface that have fallen in on themselves as a result of movements of Earth's crust. At one time there was a layer of lava at the surface; when volcanic action below opened up an underground bubble, the surface collapsed onto itself, creating several acres of pit craters. Over time, vegetation has clothed the slopes of these depressions, and the visitor sees a rich bowl of greenery.

Los Gemelos are located on either side of the road that goes between Puerto Ayora and the Itabaca Canal, between Santa Cruz and Baltra islands. It is a common destination for groups on their day in town. The attractive site is just a few minutes' walk into the open area, which is in the *Scalesia* forest zone and is rich in bird and plant life. If you're lucky, a short-eared owl (*Asio flammeus*) may be perched on one of the moss-covered *Scalesia* branches. The Park Service has established an important, difficult restoration project for the area to remove invasive plants like blackberry, which is making some progress.

CALETA TORTUGA NEGRA

This is "Black Turtle Cove," a tidal lagoon that is almost mazelike in its complex shape. It is etched into the north coast of Santa Cruz, just southwest of Baltra. The cove has a narrow entrance, reached after a brief panga ride, and then it stretches nearly a kilometer inland with its farthest end being more than half a kilometer wide. You will stay in your panga the whole time; after you have motored into the lagoon, the motor will be turned off, and the panga will be paddled quietly to avoid disturbing the wildlife.

The entrance into the lagoon is a very good place to see all three kinds of mangroves: the red (*Rhizophora mangle*), white (*Laguncularia racemosa*), and black (*Avicennia germinans*). Your guide will tell you how to distinguish one from the other. Here you can see very clearly the role mangroves play in providing habitat for a wide variety of wildlife. Oysters cling to the roots, pelicans perch on the heights, and herons pick their way along the prop roots that link the branches to the muddy bottom. Mullets flash in and out of the fingerlike roots underwater.

Once you are well into the lagoon, you are likely to be in for some very exciting

Yellow-tailed mullets feeding near the surface in a mangrove lagoon, Isabela

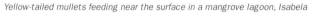

moments. The brackish, calm waters are frequented by the white-tipped shark and spotted eagle rays and golden rays. Each time I have been there I have seen a number of the sharks, sliding below the boat or gathering in the shadow of the over-hanging mangrove branches.

The rays are also an intriguing feature. The spotted eagle rays are easily a meter wide. They seem to hover at the surface and even raise their "heads" out of the water now and then.

The golden rays are smaller, and when I saw them they were traveling in groups. They are very graceful, with the smooth movement of their "wings" showing alter-nately the cream-colored underside and the dull mustard color of their backs. They are diamond shaped, and they were traveling in a diamond-shaped forma-tion. The pattern-within-a-pattern of their movement was lovely.

You might see Green Pacific marine turtles, for they gather here to mate. On one of my trips we were sitting qui-etly in the panga, when suddenly we heard a puff, a gentle, moist exhalation behind us. We turned and saw the beak of a turtle just rising from the surface of the water. Then there was another puff a few meters in the other direction, then another and another. Next we noticed the water roiling not far away. We went a bit closer, and sure enough, the back of a turtle showed, then a flipper appeared, then the paler belly and another side and back. It became obvious that this was a pair of turtles locked into a copulatory embrace. They do this for hours, gently rolling, sometimes entirely submerged, sometimes both heads appearing as they come up for air.

The experience of this lagoon brought our group of very diverse people very close together. A sense of peaceful, smil-ing affection permeated the panga as we returned to our home boat, and was sustained throughout the trip. It was an unexpected bonus to form a bond on that first day that lasted for the whole trip.

DRAGON HILL

Dragon Hill is a wonderful walk through three different environments, each rich in plant and animal life, on land and in the lagoons and the ocean. The site is on the northwestern coast of Santa Cruz where the coast is lined with black rocks, con-trasting with the bright white beach sand. There are dozens of tiny islets and rocks emerging from the water, depending on the tide. Some groups snorkel there, from their panga, before heading for the trail. Part of the trail runs beside tidepools and tiny inlets of crystal-clear water, and you can easily peer down into the marine life there (remember your polarizing filter for your camera). There are also marine igua-nas here and there, swimming, feeding, basking on the rocks.

The landing is a dry one, leading directly to a rather rocky trail. The trail is 1.6 kilometers (1 mile) long, with the first part being a bit of a scramble on red clay,

LEFT: *Large cactus finch, San Cristóbal* RIGHT: *Galapagos sulphur butterfly, Santa Cruz*

lined with rocks. You can see the Dragon Hill peak ahead of you as you climb. It is rather sharp, like a miniature Matterhorn. There is a railing to help you as you climb.

In about 10 minutes, the trail comes to a lovely lagoon. You are likely to see flamingos, quietly sieving through the mud to find the tiny shrimp (*Artemia salina*) that is their primary food, and the sources of the flamingos' pink coloration. There may be Galapagos pintail ducks there, and shorebirds such as the occasional whimbrel, black-necked stilt, or the more frequently seen sanderling.

Farther along the trail, you are in an *Opuntia* cactus "forest." These are the huge cactus with the paddle-shaped branches and the orange trunks, with oblong platelets of bark. Many have flowers, and you will see finches dipping into the yellow petals to feed. There are also palo santo trees all around, and the colorful mats of *Sesuvium* spreading across the

ground and also "climbing" among the fallen branches of palo santo and *Opuntia*. Lava lizards skitter along the trail, perch on rocks, peer and blink at visitors. On my latest visit, there was an insect bonus— close-up views of the Galapagos bee, the multicolored Galapagos grasshopper, and the Galapagos sulphur butterfly.

It is exciting to see land iguanas here. At one time they had nearly disappeared, due to predation by feral dogs. However, dogs have been eradicated, and there is constant monitoring and removal of other animal threats. After a captive breeding program for the land iguanas, the iguanas have rebounded, have been returned, and are now successfully living and reproducing here at Dragon Hill. You have a good chance of seeing them; just look carefully in the bushes, because they like the shade. You can also see many of the holes they dig for laying their eggs.

7

SITES NEAR SANTA CRUZ

Santa Cruz tends to be the pivotal point of most visitors' trips to the eastern islands of the Galapagos. As you'll see, Santa Cruz is replete with visitation opportunities, many based in the communities there. But there are many very striking, very interesting natural sites around Santa Cruz accessible via brief boat trips and fairly short visits. The easy walking trails on the uplifted island of Plaza Sur offer you your first chance to spend some time on an island formed by volcanic forces lifting whole sheets of earthen crust up into the air. You will become acquainted with lowland and shoreline plant and animal life.

Then there's Santa Fe with its treelike cactus, fed upon by the island's own species of land iguana. A short boat ride away is the gleaming white strand of Mosquera Island's beach, an easy walk, where you can peer at turtle tracks. You may even snorkel near there too. On most of these shorter rides, you will pass the almost cylindrical Daphne Major, a classic volcanic formation and home of the most intensive, prolonged study of adaptation and speciation in Darwin's finches.

Seymour Norte, another uplifted island and "sister" of Baltra, is where you may first have landed. It is one of the success stories of both rat eradication and the development of an effective captive breeding program at the national park. The babies hatched there are returned to their home island between ages three and five years. There is much to see, then, on these islands around Santa Cruz.

PLAZA SUR

Plaza Sur (South Plaza) is a small island, only 130 meters (425 feet) wide and a kilometer long, the southern of a pair of crescent-shaped islands not far off the east side of Santa Cruz. Unlike the conical volcanic islands, Plaza Sur is the result of shifts in Earth's crust, which have lifted it above the surface of the water. It is like a tilted tabletop, rising gradually from the beach to cliffs of about 20 meters (65 feet) on the south side.

Landing on the island usually is easy because there is a small cement jetty to which the panga can pull up. If the water is calm, you should be able to make a dry, though sometimes slippery, landing and then take the easy walk of about an hour. The only obstacle to landing (a momentary one) is that sea lions also love to lie on the jetty. If they really won't move at the arrival of visitors, then the guide may have to clap or make other noises to make them depart, which the sea lions do, in what seems to me to be a rather grumpy manner.

Once you are on the island, the first thing you'll notice is the vegetation. This is one of the islands with tree-sized prickly pear cactus (*Opuntia echios*). They are very handsome with their bright russet bark, textured in a mosaic of elongated diamond-shaped plates. Rising from the bark are veritable explosions of gray spines, more than 3 centimeters (about 1 inch) long. Along the branches and at their tips are great fleshy paddles. These green paddles are a source of food for the land iguanas (*Conolophus subcristatus*) that are common here. It is wonderful to see the sturdy, pink-tongued iguanas stand on their hind legs to munch on those spine-laden pads. Leathery gums seem to be their savior. The second most favored food plant for the land iguanas is *Portulaca oleracea*, a moisture-hoarding succulent, with its small, yellow flowers.

Portulaca, *Plaza Sur*

Typically, because of the extreme dryness of these low-lying islands, there are swaths of gray, rootlike vegetation in clumps and mats over their surface. In great contrast to the drab background is the brilliant rose-red of the *Sesuvium* plant, a colonizer of harsh sandy zones near the water. There are two species, which your guide can distinguish for you, that are endemic to the islands.

The *Sesuvium* has fleshy branches, as many arid zone plants do. It also is a succulent, and like the *Opuntia* and *Portulaca* it stores moisture in its fleshy parts, which are covered by a waxy exterior that retards moisture loss.

The path for Plaza Sur forms a circle in the middle of the island, running south overland, then east along the bluffs, back

Spotted rays, like these near Santa Cruz, are easier to photograph (and see) with a polarizing filter.

across the island, and then along the lower, boulder-strewn north shore. The trail is a classic example of Park Service trail design, unobtrusively marked by the little gnarled posts of local wood, painted with a band of white and black. The trail is easy to follow and goes exactly where you would want to go. As you begin the trek to the bluffs, there is a gradual incline. The sea lions are left behind, and the light yellow and gray-green land iguanas begin to appear more frequently.

Soon the path comes closer to the black, rocky cliffs. Sheer in places, crumbly in others (exercise caution here), the cliff edge is a great place for bird-watching and for peering into the clear water below. Swallow-tailed gulls (*Creagrus furcatus*) usually are there, wheeling and swooping in the incessant wind. Sometimes there

are nests with mottled gray and white young dotted along the side of the cliffs. As the gulls land against the air currents, there is usually a good opportunity to photograph them, wings outstretched, forked tails spread. No matter where they are, always stay at least 2 meters (6 feet) away from a nest.

Not landing but sometimes seen are red-billed tropicbirds (*Phaethon aethereus*) circling the island. There will be blue-footed and Nazca boobies, some of which may perch on the cliff face. Galapagos shearwaters (*Puffinus subalaris*) may be swirling over the water's surface below. Frigate birds are ever-present.

The cliff edge is a good place for spotting sea life as well. On several visits we spotted manta rays as big as a dinner table, like sailing ships just under the

surface of the water. Look for hammerhead sharks here, also. The hammerhead
is so common that it has become the symbol for the marine reserve. There were
also shoals of mullet devouring the same
plankton the mantas feed on.

On the final quarter of the walk the
trail traces the lower side of the island.
First, near the water, are some small
sandy areas lined with rocks. Marine iguanas bask and bob their heads in the sun.
Continuing on, there is even less vegetation and a lot of rocks and boulders to
pick your way through. The rocks have a
shiny white patina, the result of sea lion
bodies polishing their own excrement
year after year as they lumber over their
territory to and from the water. Watch
your step on these polished surfaces.

Plaza Sur is one of the few islands that
have been spared the ravages of introduced species or uncontrolled human
use. Other than goats and mice, there
have been no introduced animal species,
and the goats were eliminated by 1961. It
is a good way to see what an undisturbed
or fully recovered island can be like—
dense with wildlife, its natural plants
intact, its spare beauty surrounding the
visitor and the inhabitants alike.

SANTA FE

Santa Fe includes one of the few rigor-
ous trail segments of the frequently visited sites. But it also has one of the most
sheltered and beautiful anchorages of
all the ones you will stay in. This deeply
indented cove is marvelous for a quiet rest

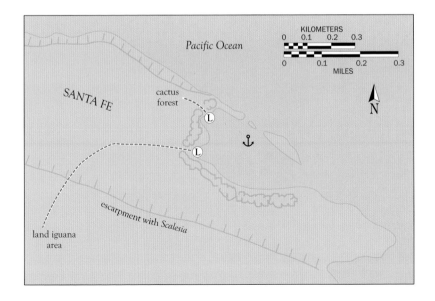

Iguana and symbiotic finch, Santiago

and swim after the slog up the cliff to see the land iguana species (*Conolophus pallidus*) that is unique to this island.

This is another uplifted island (as described in chapter 2's section on geology). Santa Fe does have traces of surface volcanic activity, however. There are remains of underwater lava flows that were uplifted as the whole island plate was pushed to the surface. Santa Fe is 17 nautical miles (31.5 kilometers or 19.6 miles) from the southeast edge of Santa Cruz, and it will take from one and a half to three hours to get there, depending on boat speed.

After a wet landing on a small sandy beach, the trail ascends gently at first, but at the base of the cliff there is a short steep ascent that takes about five minutes. The path is clear—there's nowhere else to go—but it can be crumbly and a little tiring if the temperature is already high. A helping hand from the guide or other visitors is all that's needed to reach the top.

On the way up, notice the huge *Opuntia* here and the *Scalesia* plants at the upper levels. Although *Scalesia* is associated most often with the moist uplands, there are several species that occupy the arid coastal zones. The species seen here is *Scalesia helleri*. You may notice that some of the plants on the steep slope have been tagged so that scientists can trace their development.

The trek to the top of the escarpment isn't always rewarded with a land iguana sighting, but peer carefully in the under-brush and you may be fortunate. This species is found only on this island. It is distinguished by its paler yellow color, longer, more tapered snout, unusually heavy ridge of spikes along its backbone, rather like extremely tough, pointed fin-gernails. They can move briskly, although those I saw were deeply attached to the warm earth and the only movements evi-dent were light breathing and the occa-sional eye blink. Though you will not be there to see this, at night they sleep in burrows to retain the body heat they've absorbed during the day. These land iguanas also have a working relationship (symbiotic) with the finches on the island. The finches land on the iguanas and pick off ticks and parasites and have a high-protein snack in the process.

Once you've made the trek to the escarpment and returned to the beach area, you may have time to go to the next landing site to the north. A short trail from there goes to a very fine stand of the *Opuntia* cactus (*Opuntia echios*). The brief walk is made more interesting by having to sidestep sea lions that typically loll on the beach and in the shade of nearby rocks. En route to the *Opuntia* forest our group had a rare sighting of a Galapagos snake—a sighting made even more unusual by the fact that it was ingesting a lava lizard headfirst, with half the lizard inside the snake and half out.

After you return to your boat, you will have a chance to enjoy the other highlight of Santa Fe—its beautiful cove. A long arm of rocks stretches from the beach and ends in a small island. You will be situ-ated about halfway along the arm. First check out the island itself for Galapagos hawks. They are regulars here. One night we were visited by an owl, which landed momentarily in our rigging. Pelicans are likely to be hovering around, and frigate birds will be attracted by the boat. This particular cove is a place to be at one with the water. In such a protected cove, swim-ming is easy and snorkeling is good all along the inside of the rocky arm. You'll be joined by sea lions and other creatures as well.

Santa Fe was once plagued by goats, but they were eradicated in 1971. Thus what the visitor sees is an island well on its way to recovery. It's good to know that

Pelican coming in for a landing at sea

such distinctive beauty has a real chance to continue on its natural course.

MOSQUERA

Mosquera is a playground of sand, rocks, and tidepools. Sea lions are plentiful, scattered all over the thin strip of fine white sand that is the island. The best view of Mosquera comes just as the plane is turning for its final descent to the Baltra runway. Look for the crescent of gleaming white sand; that's Mosquera flashing below you.

This is an open area for visitors. There are no fixed paths, and you will mostly be strolling along the beach, perhaps walking along the low, brushy dunes or swimming. However, it is very important to keep your distance from the sea lions, whether they are peacefully sleeping or actively playing or swimming. They can move surprisingly quickly on land and are lightning fast in the water. If there are babies, be sure not to come between a mother and the baby. The males are very territorial, and if there are males nearby, on land or out in the water "patrolling" back and forth, stay away. Your guide can point out the males, and will make sure that you stay at least 2 meters (6 feet) away or simply stay out of the water if necessary.

The rare endemic lava gull (*Larus fuliginosus*) is known to nest on tiny Mosquera, among the spare plant life or in gravelly flat areas. Being out in the open like that, they are very vulnerable to disturbances of any kind, so visitors will want to be watchful and careful not to disturb these handsome, unique birds and their next generations.

The plant life, thin and sparse, is very fragile and the same care should be taken not to trample it.

Bird-watching is good on Mosquera. Pelicans and boobies post themselves on the higher rocks, and shorebirds peck and probe at the water's edge. I saw three semipalmated plovers (*Charadrius semipalmatus*) and a sanderling (*Crocethia alba*), two old friends known to birders from North America.

DAPHNE MAJOR

Daphne Major is a small volcanic cone rising abruptly out of the sea just north of Santa Cruz and west of Baltra, and it is a frequently seen landmark. But its fragility and value to basic research on its varied birdlife have caused it to be set aside by the park, largely for scientific use. (Daphne Minor is a much smaller sibling of Daphne Major, just 6 kilometers [3.7 miles] north of it. Daphne Minor is only 0.08 square kilometer [0.03 square mile] in area, one-fourth the size of Daphne Major.) A permit from the Park Service is required to visit there, so your visit will likely be via a tour around the island by boat. There is still a lot to see from the boat, and binoculars are a must.

Daphne Major is slightly oval in shape, but from almost any direction at sea level it looks like a completely circular cone that has been lopped off crisply at the

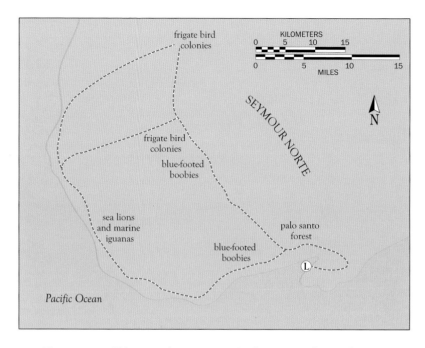

top. The crater itself has two layers: a small flat circle not far below where the trail ends, and another layer much lower. The lower level is much larger than the upper one. The blue-footed boobies nest on the bright white floors of the crater. From your panga circumnavigation of the island you will be seeing them come and go to their nests, disappearing from view as they descend. Nazca boobies nest on the outer slopes of the cone. The lovely brown noddy terns swoop in and settle into the crevices of the slopes as well.

It is also possible that you will see the red-billed tropicbird flying toward the island, because they nest in crevices in the rocky inner walls of the crater.

Daphne Major is known for its finches, in that for more than four decades they have been the objects of ornithological study of evolution. Much is now known about their reproduction and their survival patterns in the face of fluctuating moisture, food, and temperature.

SEYMOUR NORTE

Unlike the characteristically cone-shaped islands that make up most of the Galapagos, formed by the accumulation of lava and other volcanic debris, Seymour Norte (North Seymour) was formed by uplift of its rocky base from below sea level. This uplifting of Earth's crust, which sometimes brings the sea bottom high enough that it becomes dry land, is frequently found in the islands, although it is not the primary means of land building. For Seymour Norte the uplift of some ancient lava flow (formerly underwater) has resulted in terrain that is fairly flat, often with a gentle slope in one particular direction. On Seymour Norte, the slope falls gradually away from the southern side with the low cliffs that greet the visitor at the landing site.

Seymour Norte is a very busy island. Its location close by its "sister" island Baltra puts it along the route of many boats. The large boats and day-tripping and island-hopping visitors stop here. It is also a busy nesting place for blue-footed boobies and the Galapagos' largest nesting colony of magnificent frigate birds (*Fregata magnificens*). There are sea lions and swallow-tailed gulls, and maybe you'll even spot a Galapagos snake, as we did on one trip.

Land iguanas are seen all along the trail. Introduced rats were eradicated in 2007, and soon afterward baby iguanas were being noted by guides. In 1932 and 1933, seventy land iguanas from Baltra were introduced to Seymour Norte in the hope that these animals were more likely to survive here than on Baltra, which was already populated by introduced goats, cats, etc. In 1980, two adult land iguanas from Seymour Norte were taken to the breeding center on Santa Cruz, one of the first efforts of a program of reproduction and rearing of land iguanas in captivity. These were used to rebuild the population on Baltra. This effort, combined with a successful introduced rat eradication project, means that the land iguana population on Seymour Norte is quite robust.

If your panga ride to disembark on Seymour Norte includes a short side trip along the face of the cliffs of the island, it can be a very rich wildlife adventure. You can see how the swallow-tailed gulls perch on the rocky edges, waiting for night and their time to feed; have a close view of the many sea lions, with their young ones lounging in the tidepools; and have close-up views of the black, polygonal basaltic columns of rock that form the cliffs.

The landing can be difficult, depending on the size of the ocean swell. It's a short leap, aided by a crew member, onto a landing jetty. The one frustration at the landing point may be that—right there—you might see some swallow-tailed gulls. (They like rock-strewn cliffs, and these low ones have a certain appeal.) Then you may be torn between trying to watch your footing, not holding up anyone behind you, and trying to take some pictures very quickly. (You'll probably get a more leisurely look at them on Plaza Sur.)

At first glance, this is one of the most nondescript islands to be visited. The variety of palo santo tree (*Bursera malacophylla*) found on Seymour Norte and Daphne Major, endemic to those two islands, is hairier and more stunted than its taller relatives. Otherwise you'll see flat

Great frigate father and fluffy chick

ground, with gray saltbush (*Cryptocarpus pyriformis*) distributed here and there, and some slightly more open areas with bird guano–splashed rocks. At the beach area there may be young sea lions resting in what shade they can find.

Then, nearly at your feet, you may see your first blue-footed booby at its nest, cocking its golden eye at you, with perhaps a couple of eggs showing beneath it. Or maybe you'll see an ugly, gray, nearly naked bag of avian entrails under a shading wing. (It's the whole chick, but in their earliest days they seem to be made mostly of bulbous gut and knife-edge beak.)

If there is nesting going on, you will almost certainly be treated to some fantastic displays. The blue feet play a major role in choosing a mate, setting up the nest, leaving that nest to feed or loaf, and returning to it without setting off antagonism or fear. The boobies dip and bow, spread their wings, turn and twist them, and paddle their feet to show them off to best advantage. Lots of whistling and honking go on as well.

It's not only the adults that do this, either. I have seen young still clothed in down, with only their wings fully feathered, engage in the same types of bowing, wing spreading, and tail tipping. Is it practice for the future or just avian fun?

It will be hard to move on from there, even though the birds are nearly oblivious to you, but there's a lot more to follow, for in a few minutes you come to the nesting grounds of the magnificent frigate bird.

Seymour Norte hosts the largest colony of nesting great frigate birds in the islands. A few magnificent frigates nest there as well. Frigates are large and aggressive birds. They are known as a "klepto-parasite," living off of the work of other birds, stealing their catch from them after vigorous chases in the sky. They have a wingspan of more than 2 meters (6 feet) and are consummate flyers. In fact, it is hard to believe that a bird that big can be so quick on its wings.

These huge birds build their scruffy nests on the tops of bushes at the farthest extent of the trail (which is a two-part loop, with the fullest extent being about 3.2 kilometers [2 miles] long). If a male does not have a mate yet, he will sit on a nest and watch the females wheeling over. As one comes close overhead he may throw out his wings to their fullest extent, throw back his head, puff out his garish red throat pouch, and shake himself in a frenzy of invitation (though the pouch may be puffed up or deflated seemingly at any other time, as can be often seen when they are flying overhead). It is the decision of the female that finalizes the formation of a pair.

Once a pair has established themselves, whichever one of them is at the nest sits there quietly for the most part, particularly if they already have an egg or chick to care for. The parents take turns feeding or brooding the young, which, except for their long hook-tipped bills, look like they will never grow up to be what their parents are. They are a brilliant fluffy white until they are nearly the size of the parents. It takes months of careful nurturing for them to look and act like the patient adult birds that care for them.

The trail also takes you along a narrow strip of pure white sand on the lower edge of the island. The sand wends its way between the more inland vegetation and the shoreline rocks. The walk is short here but very beautiful. You can go to the rocks and pools where the sea lions are or stay on the sand, and then turn inland on the trail that leads into vegetation.

On your way out, if you have been going counterclockwise on the trail, you will be near the cliffs again. Along the beach you may spot sea lions, and in the bushes near the shore you may spy a Galapagos snake. This is their home also.

8

SANTIAGO

Santiago's numerous visitor sites and its location in the center of the archipelago make it one of the most familiar islands of a Galapagos visit. You go from site to site on Santiago, learning about the human history of the islands and seeing the fur seals or Galapagos hawks. Some of the shoreline was created by lava flows only about a century ago. You will take a quick jaunt to Bartolomé's Pinnacle Rock (see chapter 9) or pull into the quiet cove of Sombrero Chino (see chapter 10) for a brief but lovely trail and some snorkeling. But wherever you go around the island, the cone of Santiago's Sugarloaf volcano or the sweep of black volcanic rock on its shores will appear again and again, giving you a visual anchor for a major part of your visit.

This island has powerful evocations of past human use, although with eradication of goats complete, it is now recovering from this scourge, and also healing from several attempts at salt mining.

It also has some of the most impressive natural sites: the fur seal grottoes and the geologically recent lava flows at Sulivan Bay (named by *Beagle* captain Robert FitzRoy to honor a young shipmate, who in later life became Sir Bartholomew James Sulivan, 1810–1890).

In visiting Santiago and nearby sites, you'll find bird-watching particularly rewarding, with sightings of Galapagos hawks, or even vermilion flycatchers—if you're fortunate. Migrating shorebirds are seen regularly also.

Santiago is an important example of successful eradication of introduced species, with pigs eradicated in 2006. The removal of the goat population in 2009 left the island largely without herbivores. While the elimination of goats is so very important, there was then a new kind of environmental imbalance as plant life developed dramatically, including both endemic and invasive plants. This in turn seemed to be linked to a substantial increase in rats, as

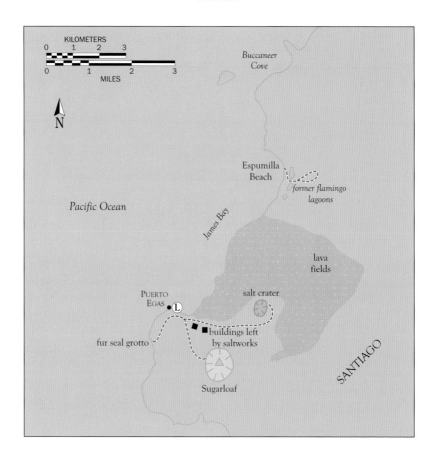

indicated by higher proportions of rats in the diet of the endemic Galapagos hawk. However, more rats can negatively affect ground-nesting birds. What all of this shows is that conservation programs in the Galapagos are designed to be as multifaceted and long-term as possible, since no one component (e.g., goat eradication) is the whole answer to recovery of any one or more valued endemic species.

JAMES BAY

This bay, on the northwest side of Santiago, is a lovely stopping place in itself, but its chief function is the starting point for three visitor sites: the salt crater, the fur seal grottoes, and Espumilla Beach. The first two are reached from the same anchorage, and Espumilla Beach is a short boat ride to the northern end of the bay.

James Bay usually offers a particularly good chance to savor the sea life around you. If you are there in the early morning or later afternoon, sit on deck and watch what goes on around the boat. The blue-footed boobies plunge for fish, and the pelicans dive and then swim along the surface, followed closely by the brown noddy terns, who hope that fish will spill out of the pelicans' pouches. Sometimes a noddy even sits on a pelican's head to be really close to the action. Sally Lightfoot crabs scuttle over the exposed black rocks near the shoreline. (They're especially easy to see on the one rock protruding fingerlike, above the surface near the point where you will disembark.)

When I was there in the severe El Niño event of 1982–83, this anchorage was the place where I saw the most storm petrels (*Oceanodroma castro*) at once, flitting and dipping over the water's surface as they fed. The water was so calm that in the flat light of evening it gleamed as though dark oil had been poured on it. Only these tiny birds, themselves nearly completely black, relieved the unbroken somberness as I peered down onto the water.

Fur seal grotto established in a collapsed lava tube, Santiago

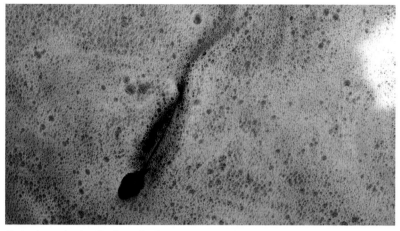

Marine iguana in shoreline foam, Santiago

PUERTO EGAS AND THE SALT CRATER

After a wet landing, you'll walk a few dozen meters (100 to 150 feet) to the area used in the 1920s and again in the 1960s as a port for a salt extraction operation. At first, as you begin your walk, the view is rather bleak. There is a collection of rusted hulks of old machinery and the remains of posts from defunct sheds. It is known that this area was first visited in 1683, and there have been sporadic visits over the centuries by those wanting to fish in the bay or to use the salt for preserving meat and fish, but now the interest in the salt is strictly historic, as the guides will explain.

The trail is about 8 kilometers (5 miles) long, out-and-back (not a loop), and will take about three hours to do. It actually follows the remnants of a wagon road once used to haul the salt, winding away from the shore and up around the slopes of the crater's cone. It's hard to get much of a sense of the topography at first; there's just a slope on your left side and flat ground to the immediate right.

It's an easy walk, although on a very hot day it can seem a lot longer than it is. Wear shoes, not sandals; lightweight slacks also are a good idea. Somehow this hike seems to be one of the hottest excursions. To minimize discomfort, keep a close eye on the sights along the trail, and don't be too impatient to reach the rim of the salt crater itself.

As the elevation gradually increases, the bird-watchers in the group probably will have some great moments. The slope of the crater is a likely place to see the vermilion flycatcher. This bird contrasts beautifully here with the stark dark gravel at your feet and the gray palo santo trees that clothe the slopes of Santiago. The bird will be sitting on a branch, head and chest red beyond imagining, and then it will launch itself out into the air to snap at an insect too small and too fast for a human eye to see. The click of its bill as it makes the catch is how you'll know he's succeeded (or she, if it is the more subtly colored buff-and-brown female). Then the bird circles back to its original perch, having completed a circle perhaps a meter in diameter.

With luck, you will see the large-billed flycatcher (Myarchus magnirostris), too. Its colors are not as spectacular, but its similar feeding habits are just as interesting. I have found them to be quite unfazed by observers and quite easy to photograph.

The trail usually is rich with finches. I saw the warbler finch here once, and the famous woodpecker finch, the dream of anyone interested in bird behavior. For me it happened as I noticed a bird that seemed to be pecking into a tree. I wondered, "Could it be?" As I went closer, I saw that it was holding in its beak what looked like a cactus spine about an inch long. It was using the spine to probe into the tree. It was indeed the woodpecker finch! I was actually seeing something that I'd read about and seen in films and here it was, a bird using a tool! Then the finch dropped that spine and came back with a wobbly-looking twig, very thin and crooked. The bird tried probing with it a couple of times, to no avail because the twig bent. So it dropped that one and went off to another tree that had

thorns and picked one of those. That one seemed to work.

At the rim of the salt crater are marvelous sights on both sides. First is the crater itself. Its volcano is long extinct, and its floor is about 10 meters (32 feet) below sea level. Evidently salt water seeps in slowly through cracks in the rock; as it comes up in the crater itself, a shallow, briny lake is formed. The fierce sun evaporates the surface water and the remains can be collected as usable salt. Several efforts have been made to create a viable business of this, one as late as the 1960s, but none succeeded. (Of course, such an enterprise would be prohibited in today's national park.)

Depending on the level of water in the salt crater, it's possible at times to see remains of sections of the partitions placed in the lake to control the water level to speed up further drying of the salt. The outlines of these still cut the circular lake into pie-shaped wedges. The edges usually are a brilliant white, and the center may be white, tan, bright green, or even reddish, depending on the water level and the growth of algae. Look closely for a flamingo or two in the distance; you may be lucky.

You will be seeing here a scene that Darwin described in his *Voyage of the Beagle*. He reported,

One day we accompanied a party of the Spaniards in their whale-boat to a Salina, or lake from which salt is

procured. After landing, we had a very rough walk over a rugged field of recent lava, which has almost surrounded a tuff-crater, at the bottom of which the salt-lake lies.

The water is only three or four inches deep, and rests on a layer of beautifully crystallized, white salt. The lake is quite circular, and is fringed with a border of bright green succulent plants; the almost precipitous walls of the crater are clothed in wood, so that the scene was altogether both picturesque and curious. A few years since, the sailors belonging to a sealing vessel murdered their captain in this quiet spot, and we saw his skull lying among the bushes.

These days visitors aren't allowed to go down into the crater to see whether the skull is still there or to see the salt crystals up close, but you will see clearly from the rim, across the other side of the crater, the remains of the road constructed for the more recent salt extraction attempts, starting at the salt pan level. Now it's just a pale gash, gracefully winding up and around half of the crater's interior slope.

If you turn in the other direction, looking directly away from the crater's center, you face wave upon wave of black and orange lava fields. These vast sweeps of ground of contrasting color very much characterize the vistas on the island. The older flows—the orange ones—have a fair amount of vegetation scattered over

them. The stark gray of the palo santo trees is broadcast over the orange slopes as far as the eye can see. The more recent black flows seem utterly barren, and only a much closer examination allows the visitor to see that even here, plant and animal life exist.

THE FUR SEAL GROTTOES

The fur seal grottoes are only a 750-meter (half a mile) walk from the same landing used for the salt crater. The level, sandy trail is off to the right, roughly following the edge of the island but a few meters in from the somewhat rocky shore. The trail here is very good for bird-watching. There may be Galapagos hawks; often there are shorebirds feeding on tidbits along the wave-splashed rocks.

On almost all of my visits I have seen oystercatchers (*Haematopus ostralegus*), most impressive with their black and white plumage, red bills, yellow-ringed eyes, and stubby pink feet. Three whimbrels flew overhead on one of my visits, and finches are common in the nearby brush. In places, the rocks are also packed with marine iguanas. Quite often they are piled on each other in layers, two or even three deep. This is one of their strategies for retaining body heat. They seem to compete with each other for the spot that has the most direct exposure to the sun, even if it means clinging nearly vertically from a shoreline boulder with tails hanging out into space.

A whimbrel, an international migrant, Santa Cruz

The walk is an easy 15 minutes, ending at a small plain of black lava flow. This area is pocked by three potholes. These holes are formed in the same way that the Santa Cruz lava tubes were formed, only these grottoes are not land-locked. The lava flow went out to the open sea, and now the water rushes in and out of the tubes with the tides. The tops of the tubes have caved in here and there, making the open pothole that you look down into. At one time, visitors could swim in these grottoes, but the combination of risks to swimmers of surging tides and possible disturbance to the wildlife has closed this option.

The main two pools are a beautiful sight, however, connected as they are to each other with a bridge of black lava arching over them near the middle of their length. The exit of the pool to the open sea also has an arch over it, where it's great just to sit and watch the water flow back and forth below you.

You'll have company here. The fur seals can often be seen lounging around at the

Sea lion pup and marine iguanas, Santiago

edges of the pools. They plunge into the water now and then, and there also will be sea lions swishing below with total ease and nonchalance.

The grottoes are only about 15 meters (50 feet) long, but for sheer beauty and ease of access, few places on the island can compete with their black rocks, crystal-clear blue water, fur seals, and tropical fish. On almost every one of my many visits, I saw what I like to think is the same yellow-crowned night heron on exactly the same rock, just a step below the rim of the largest pool. It was like some welcoming sign, confirming for the visitor that all was well.

ESPUMILLA BEACH

Espumilla Beach, at the northern shore of James Bay, has historic significance. Just north of it is a source of fresh water,

much prized by pirates who plied these waters centuries ago. Now visitors go there for the quiet beach and the birdlife in the vegetation lining the beach. I've seen black-necked stilts (*Himantopus mexicanus*) and white-cheeked pintails (*Anas bahamensis galapagensis*) in the freshwater lagoons that sometimes form behind the dunes.

A 2-kilometer (1.25-mile) trail goes inland from the beach. It makes a slight ascent over a knob of land and then loops back to its starting point. There are several finch species to see, and perhaps vermilion flycatchers.

BUCCANEER COVE

Buccaneer Cove is less than an hour's sail north of James Bay and Espumilla Beach. It is not a visitor site as such, and your boat may just sail into the cove so your guide can tell you about its human history. That history is fascinating and important, but be sure to take a good look at the scenery; the cliff walls in particular are spectacular.

The cove served generations of pirates and then whalers as a safe harbor near one of the few freshwater sources in the islands. They would land, take on water, collect some tortoises for fresh meat, and gather firewood for the ship's galley. Remains of earthenware storage vessels have been found submerged offshore where they were dumped when empty.

Seeing the cove can give you a few vicarious chills at the thought of these men, living at the edges of human law and their own physical endurance. But it also can give you a very immediate sense of awe as you look up at the vast, vertical walls, especially on the north side, that encompass much of the cove. The cove is the remnant of a volcano that formed at the edge of the island. You can trace the layers upon layers of volcanic debris that have been deposited over time. Sometimes explosions expelled tons of fine materials, which settled back around the central vent and built up the walls of the crater. Other layers are composed of molten lava that pushed up more slowly and partially filled the crater's depths.

Wind, rain, and the invading ocean have eroded the cove walls to leave some of the most dramatic scenery in the Galapagos. On the south wall in particular are the multihued strata that tell of

the cone's growth and erosion. All along the north wall there are great pockmarks, caves, and fingerlike vertical protrusions. Here the wall's deep browns and buffy yellows are splashed with the white of bird excrement, an undignified source of lovely visual accents. And frigate birds and blue-footed boobies sit peering out to sea or launch themselves out for a fishing sortie. Your boat may come very close to the wall to give you a good view. The closeness may be a bit nerve-racking, but your guide probably will explain that the cliffs are as perpendicular below the surface as above and that the water there is very deep indeed. So be sure to be out on deck with binoculars and camera, and be ready to take in these brief but spectacular moments.

SULIVAN BAY LAVA FLOWS

As your boat passes by Santiago on its various trips and as it pulls into Sulivan Bay itself, you often see wedges of black lava cutting across the island's reddish slopes. Santiago is a classic volcanic island, rising to a dominant cone nearly 1000 meters (3280 feet) tall at its northwest side. It also has many smaller cones projecting from its major slope, some with craters and others not.

Sulivan Bay is the place to be reminded of how active the volcanic land building is in the Galapagos. The lava flow for this site occurred in 1897. It is a great swath of lava that oozed down to the sea, curling around small tuff cones that were already

Pahoehoe lava flow, Santiago

there, adding land at the sea's edge where there was no land before. There is a lot to be learned here about land-building processes, but first comes the feeling of astonishment and mystery as you walk over the shiny black lava fields.

The landing is a dry one onto a small ledge or a wet one onto the shore. Be sure to bring lightweight running shoes to protect your feet. As you enter the lava field, what looks from a distance to be monotonous paving turns out to be a multilevel terrain of sheer fascination. At first you will be walking on what seems to be a kind of immobile black batter—110 square kilometers (42.5 square miles) of it. The proper name for this kind of flow is *pahoehoe*, pronounced with five syllables ("pa-HO-ay-HO-ay"), the Hawaiian word for "ropey." Used by scientists everywhere

to describe the same type of lava flow and surface character, it is an apt word, conveying very well the shapes the lava takes as it flows fairly slowly, hardening into fans and swirls and protrusions of roughly parallel rope-shaped strands. The contrasting surface areas, seen now and then here and in other lava flows you will visit, are very rough, resulting from explosive lava eruptions forcing their way through the slower-flowing lava. This gritty, sharp lava form is called *a-a*, pronounced "ah-ah."

This kind of pattern is formed when the superheated lava cools more rapidly on its surface than in its interior. The lower, hotter part continues to flow and the upper parts begin to drag as they cool and harden. This uneven cooling gives the flowing mass its characteristic fan shape, with a series of curving creases roughly perpendicular to the direction of the flow. The flatness of the land over which the lava flows allows it to separate and flow around obstacles such as earlier-established volcanic cones. The fact that this rate of flow is slow, rather than being the result of explosive volcano-building, allows the flow to meander. There are fans of the lava that are a few inches in diameter as well as ones several meters across; they all interweave and overlap in the most marvelous fashion.

There are various levels of this huge gleaming surface, evidently because of the buildup of gases below, which could raise a section and then let it drop as the gas cooled. There are some very large cracks where you can see down to other layers of rock; the average depth of the whole field is 1.5 meters (5 feet). Some cracks take a bit of a jump to get across, or you can just follow the crack to its end and keep going in a slightly different direction. There are also strings of bubbles, surface "streams" broken at their tops, and you can see knee-high mini-craters called *hornitos* ("little ovens"). These were formed when molten lava pushed its way up cracks in the hardening surface of the flows that became pahoehoe fans. It is important not to walk over parts of the flow that are clearly fragile, such as the bubbles, because such damage changes the nature and appearance of the site and is irreparable.

As you walk, think what it would have been like when the lava here began to flow, to hear and smell and see it coming

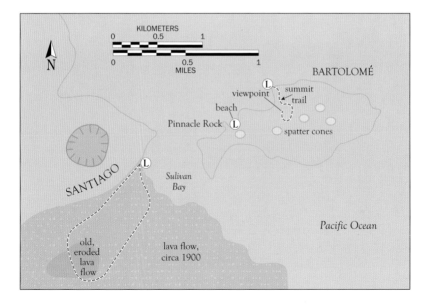

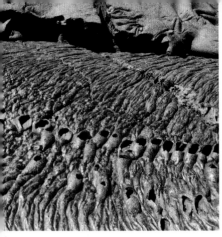

LEFT: *Burst lava bubbles* RIGHT: *Lava lizard munching on a grasshopper, Santiago*

toward you. Was it fast, or would it have been easy to step out of its path and head for the safety of that low hillock? No one was there at the time, but someone might be next time.

Another intriguing part of this flow is the plant life, past and present. Where the flowing lava encountered a plant, especially a woody section of one, it flowed around and quickly vaporized the encased plant. However, in a few cases the plant lasted long enough to leave a clear imprint, sometimes completely in the round (or hollow) of its shape. There is something eerie about this quick immortalizing process.

The lava flow also is a lesson in plant colonization. The flow is so recent, the rock so hard, and the rainfall so scarce that there is almost no organic material, much less true soil. Yet plants are scattered here and there on the stark surface. The most obvious plant is the lava cactus (*Brachycereus nesioticus*). It looks like a

fistful of very prickly cucumbers joined together at the base and then fanning outward and upward for 10 to 25 centimeters (4 to 10 inches) or so. The growing tips tend to be a bright straw color, with the older base being dark gray.

The other early colonizer of the nearly soil-less lava flow is the carpetweed plant (*Mollugo flavescens*). It forms a network of wispy stems that hug the surface of the lava and spread out only 15 or 20 centimeters (6 to 8 inches). Sometimes its tiny flowers are visible.

If there is little plant life to be seen here, there is even less animal life. There may be a very colorful grasshopper (*Schistocerca melanocera*) or so, but for the most part, flies and lava lizards are just about it, the latter preying on the former.

As you are arriving or leaving the landing area, don't forget to peer out over the water. Watch for penguins near there—you may be lucky enough to see some.

9

BARTOLOMÉ AND PINNACLE ROCK

If the giant tortoise is the wildlife emblem of the Galapagos Islands, Bartolomé and the adjoining Pinnacle Rock are surely the scenic symbols. If you saw just one photograph of the islands before you came, it probably was of this place, with Pinnacle Rock towering over an isthmus, and perfect blue-water coves on both sides. The beaches are copper-colored, and the whole scene is set off by the rugged profile of Santiago not far in the distance.

There are two sites on this small island: a hike up an extinct lava cone for a sweeping view of the nearby islands, and a beach where snorkeling and bird-watching can be very good.

SUMMIT TRAIL

The landing for the summit trail is a dry one, with visitors stepping directly from the panga onto a rock-and-concrete stairway from water level. The trail is 600 meters (2000 feet) one way. It is a

wonderfully designed and sturdily constructed boardwalk, built to preserve the fragile tuff cone surface from the erosion of thousands of visitor feet. The boardwalk steps are easy to manage, wide and not too high. There are several points where you can pause and look out at the increasingly spectacular view as you make the ascent.

All along the walk, you will be struck by the stark beauty around you. The gracefulness of the contours contrasts with the near-barrenness of the slope on which you climb. As you look closer, you will see the little lava lizards scampering across the ground or sitting on one of the small boulders that were blasted out of the throat of the now-extinct volcano that formed the island.

Scattered at distant but regular intervals are wispy plants, spreading themselves out to maximize access to moisture. They serve an important function in these conditions by stabilizing the ground

Stairway to the high point on Bartolomé, which has views of spatter cones

in which they put down their roots. The two spreading ones are *Chamaesyce amplexicaulis*, which has greenish stems, and *Tiquilia nesiotica*, the more thinly spreading of the two, which has grayish stems. And you will see that early colonizer of these bone-dry surfaces, the lava cactus (*Brachycereus nesioticus*). It looks like a very spiny cucumber, darker near its roots and its growing tips are a dull yellow.

As you follow the path, you soon come to a number of spatter cones on both sides of the trail. These are very large intrusions of lava through the gravelly tuff slopes, composed of gritty volcanic ash from previous eruptions. Some of the cones are flat at the top, with mini-craters within. Some rise up 5 or 10 meters (16 or 33 feet), with one side having been broken or eroded away. They are strikingly colored, with deep reds

and iridescent blacks and deep greens blending into each other.

Near the top you can see that the island has dozens of these cones in various stages of erosion. There are lava tubes, too, in differing sizes and various states of preservation. They look like twisting tram lines from far above. Overall, the island can make you feel as if you are on the surface of the moon, with craters scattered in every direction. The surrounding ocean is so clear that you can see more cones submerged near the shore, and you realize that the bay itself is an underwater crater, somewhat larger than many of those dotting the land. The geology of this area is so fascinating and the scenery so stark that I was told by a geologist in the group that this visit is second only to a trip to Mars.

The wind picks up as you reach the very top of the island, so come prepared

These sturdy steps on Bartolomé minimize wear and tear.

with a windbreaker. The viewing platform is large enough for visitors to spread out a bit, and you can stand and peer out in comfort, taking time to do so. This viewpoint is one of the best places in all of the Galapagos to get a strong sense of the sheer number and variety of the islands, large and small. The nearest island you can see is Santiago, a few minutes away by boat. South are Santa Cruz, Baltra, and Seymour Norte. Rábida is to the southwest. And there are dozens of islets and large rocks protruding from the ocean's surface.

The larger islands are dramatically colored, with the typical orange base, the sweeps of black lava, and the fringes of gray plant life. The ocean's color ranges from nearly white at shorelines to turquoise to blue and gunmetal gray. The profiles of the land, the contours and dimensions,

are endlessly fascinating and beautiful. Pinnacle Rock (about 70 meters [230 feet] high) at the mouth of the Bartolomé cove sets off the scene admirably. The top of the island is very far above it, and you can easily see the frigate birds that use it as a roost between their raids on other birds. Pelicans and boobies may take a rest on the Pinnacle's many small ledges also.

Keep an eye on the water farther out, too. On one of my visits huge manta rays were leaping out of the water, turning somersaults as they emerged.

Naturally you'll want your camera. Polarizing filters are a must here. There is likely to be very strong glare, whether the day is clear or overcast. For portraying the scenery, you'll want to be able to range from wide-angle to the equivalent of a 200-millimeter lens. More powerful telephoto lenses aren't particularly relevant.

THE BARTOLOMÉ BEACHES

There is an easy but wet landing at the beach at Bartolomé. The landing is on the north side of a narrow neck of land that stretches between the larger section of the island—where you probably just climbed to the top—and the smaller section, from which Pinnacle Rock soars. From the shore there is a 100-meter (330 foot) walk over the dunes to the beach on the far side. Of interest on the walk are the plants that take hold on the upper reaches of many Galapagos beaches. There are the red and white mangrove, saltbush, beach morning glory, and prickly pear with its oval paddles and spiny surfaces. The path is not wide, but it is clear and you won't have to dodge too many spines or brushy slaps in the face.

On the south side you may have a view of sea turtles if it is their nesting season (January to March); this is one of the beaches where they lay their eggs. You will be able to explore most of this beach. However, you are not allowed in the water, so that you won't disturb the variety of wildlife often found near the shore (sharks, turtles, various rays). Your guide will help you spot where turtles have laid eggs under the sand, and you will be able to go around them. Those turtles don't need any more problems with survival than they have already, so tread carefully.

There may be great blue herons stalking along the shoreline. It is also worthwhile to give a careful squint down into the water, for it is not uncommon to see hammerhead, black-tipped, and white-tipped sharks cruising the shallows.

Back at the north beach, you probably will have a chance to go swimming. The cove is an excellent spot for snorkeling; the submerged rocks and underwater ridges have a wide variety of marine life. And you are still quite near shore and in fairly shallow water.

Don't forget to look on the rocky shore near the Pinnacle for some penguins. There may be two or three, and they are wonderful to see. But do keep a distance from them, tempting though it may be to come nearer or to linger nearby. If you aren't swimming, your guide may take you on a panga ride around the Pinnacle point, and you may see penguins along the rocks there or swimming nearby.

10

SITES NEAR SANTIAGO

On Santiago, like Santa Cruz, you will visit many sites on the island, but there are also several important sites nearby. Sombrero Chino is a tiny island; from a distance, you will see how it earned its name, which translates as "Chinese hat," for the broad-brimmed hat Chinese workers around the world have traditionally worn to protect themselves from the elements. Here you will visit a quiet beach, often strolling near a group of lazing sea lions. The plant life is fascinating; various species cling to the tiny wisps of soil that have managed to find a place to land and develop enough for plants to take hold. Tiny Rábida is known for its bright reddish beaches. Behind them is a lagoon, where you may spy flamingos feeding and see sea lions napping in the shade of the mangrove bushes.

The island of Genovesa is at the far northeastern corner of the Galapagos, a trip worthwhile for visiting intriguing Darwin Bay and for walking up Prince Philip's Steps. Heaven for birders, the tidepools and shoreline plant life often harbor endemic and migratory birds. After you climb the prince's stairway, you'll be in the midst of breeding grounds for Nazca, blue-footed, and red-footed boobies. The latter are the ones most likely to engage you—they nest in the high bushes; look up to see them using their pronounced toenails on their bright feet to firmly grip their perches, swaying in the island breezes.

SOMBRERO CHINO

A visit to this small island is likely to be easygoing and comfortable. Sombrero Chino ("Chinese hat") is just 200 meters (650 feet) away from the southeast coast of Santiago, not far from the group of small islands called Bainbridge Rocks. The island is nestled in a protective curve of Santiago's shore, and this creates a quiet channel for boats to anchor in. Your boat may stay there more than once because of the island's location on the crossroads between the much-visited islands of Santa Cruz and Santiago and because it is a refuge if the sea is stormy.

For the landing on Sombrero Chino, the panga will take you to a lovely crescent-shaped beach with bright white sand. It's a wet landing but not difficult. Right away you may be among sea lions, lolling as they do on the beach or on the sandy patches scattered along the rocky shore.

The trail is only about 350 meters (1150 feet) long, following the shoreline but slightly inland. It ends at a very rocky point where waves crash in a spectacular fashion. The path is close to the shore and is an easy walk, although sturdy shoes are a good idea because of the intermittent rockiness.

The volcanic origin of the island is very clear. There are the remains of several types of lava flows here and numerous small lava tubes, some only centimeters in diameter. Many are broken and rather rough to walk on. There are patches of pahoehoe lava, the smooth, ropey type, very black and shiny. In tiny pockets that have accumulated a bit of soil, you will see one of the early colonizers of lava flows, the plant *Sesuvium edmonstonei*. Its leaves are thick and fleshy and look more like branching stems than the leaves on shrubs in moister environments. In the driest time of the year the leaves are a rose color that almost glows against the black rock. The stems hug the rock as they

branch out 40 to 50 centimeters (16 to 20 inches).

The shoreline has a number of rocky protrusions that are much loved by pelicans. You should have some great chances to photograph them. The shore itself is very rich, teeming with Sally Lightfoot crabs. How their brilliant oranges and blues stand out against the wet, black rocks!

On the inland side is the "hat" itself, rising above you with its rust-red sides, punctuated by the light grays of the palo santo trees and of the ground-hugging and wispy shrub, *Tiquilia nesiotica*. The low light of early morning or late evening seems to bring out the best of the contrasting colors of rock and plant on the slopes of the now-silent volcano.

Sombrero Chino is also an excellent place for some snorkeling. You will likely have good views, and some close proximity with sea lions, penguins, feeding marine iguanas, maybe a white-tipped shark, and certainly a multitude of colorful fish.

RÁBIDA

At first glance, Rábida is another typical beach-plus-mangrove-plus-flamingo lagoon site. But what makes it very different and very memorable is the color of the beach and island soil: a rich russet that gleams in the sun and gives everything on it a special soft beauty. The reddish hue comes from the oxidation of the iron-rich lava that is the basis of its soil. There is a short walk inland to a lovely brackish lagoon,

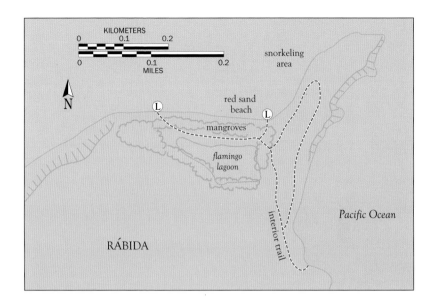

and an easy 1.6-kilometer (1-mile) loop trail among the cliff side of the island.

Rábida is small, a little more than 2 kilometers (1.25 miles) across at its widest point. It is steep and rugged and rises to more than 400 meters (1300 feet) at its highest point, although the visitor will be staying at the lowest elevations. The vegetation on the slopes consists mainly of Opuntia cactus, palo santo trees, and other scrubby bushes. Right at the shoreline is the band of mangrove that separates the beach from the saltwater lagoon that is inland just a few meters.

This is a wet landing, disembarking onto the narrow strip of beach. Usually a number of sea lions are on the beach or in the small caves that have been formed in the cliffs at the water's edge.

Even if you do not see sea lions basking or swimming at the beach, your nose will tell you whether they are still to be found a little farther on. Be careful when you walk into the mangrove strip, because the sea lions also love to sleep in the shade of the bushes. It is entirely possible to unexpectedly step on an extended flipper. An irritated sea lion can move amazingly quickly and inflict quite a bite, so caution is called for.

It takes only a minute or two to reach the lagoon. With any luck there will be flamingos sieving through the brackish water for the minute plant and animal life that they depend on for food. Each time I have been there we also saw several of the Galapagos white-cheeked pintail ducks. This is a very attractive bird with a steel-blue bill decorated by fuchsia stripes along its lower length. There have also been some recent sightings of the vermilion flycatcher here.

The inland trail is a circular route up a slight slope to a cliff overlooking a small ocean inlet. It is a little more than 2 kilometers (1.25 miles) round-trip. The path leads to an excellent view of a tiny cove; its white sandy bottom and blue waters are set in the frame of the red cliffs on which you stand. You will have a lovely stroll among the palo santo trees, and there are some sweeping views of the ocean from the low cliffs that the trail approaches. There is always the lovely contrast of red soil, blue water, white sea floor, and gray-green vegetation.

GENOVESA

Genovesa is a small island (10.5 square kilometers, 4 square miles) at the upper right-hand corner of the Galapagos archipelago. It is not visited as often as the more central islands because of the length of the voyage and the possibility of rough seas. There are two visitor sites on the island: the beach and tidepool area around Darwin Bay, and the inland area reached from the bay by Prince Philip's Steps. Both sites are particularly good for seeing interesting birdlife.

Darwin Bay

After an easy wet landing, you'll have a short walk up the brilliant white coral beach to an intriguing area of inland tidepools and rugged outcroppings of black rock several meters high. The greenery edging the pools is the saltbush (*Cryptocarpus pyriformis*), or "monte salado," as it is known in Spanish. These pools are feeding sites for migratory shorebirds such as wandering tattlers,

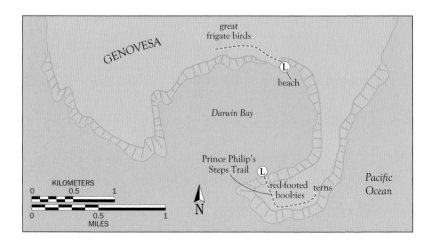

Great frigate bird on its nest with its gular pouch inflated, Genovesa

turnstones, whimbrels, oystercatchers, and semipalmated plovers. There are also the endemic lava gulls and swallow-tailed gulls. The lava gulls nest on the cliffs on the west side of the bay, and the swallow-tailed gulls nest on the cliffs of the eastern side. Yellow-crowned, lava, and black-crowned night herons are found there, too, although the latter are fairly rare.

Although warblers certainly are not considered to be shorebirds, it is common to see the yellow warbler probing along the edges of the tidepools for the little fiddler crabs and other minute shore life. The trail leaves the shore area and ascends to higher ground, where there are the nests of great frigate birds (*Fregata minor*), and if you

are there in breeding season, the sight is spectacular. You'll see the males sitting on scraggly nests with their 1.75-meter (8-foot) wingspan extended to its fullest, their scarlet gular sacs distended, voices gobbling as they peer upward, waiting for a female to choose them for a mate. If she is interested, she lands on a nearby bush and mating may or may not proceed from there.

At most times when you are likely to be visiting, there will be lots of activity: tourists fanned by breezes, birds sitting on eggs or feeding their young. But when I was in Darwin Bay during the 1982–83 El Niño, the most severe since records of this phenomenon have been kept (1958), I noted in my journal:

At that time the temperature on land that morning must have been at least 30°C [86°F] with nearly 100-percent humidity (and not raining). We could hardly keep walking; there was no breeze behind the huge boulders that lined that part of the bay.

The frigates were suffering as well. Many of them were sitting in the most grotesque positions, apparently trying to maximize their cooling. Some sat hunched on a branch, heads drooping very far down on chests, wings turned with the underside out. Others sat on the nearly vertical sides of rocks, with heads up and tails spread out almost like shovels, and their wings were bent so that they looked like they had their "arms" akimbo, also exposing the inner lining of the wings.

Some of the birds were on nests, although there were no young in sight. With these huge birds and their contorted postures, the glaring of white sand and black rock, and the heat that seemed to be baking our brains, this visit had a nightmarish quality, as though we were on the edge of delirium. Even the water was too warm to offer real relief.

It's a lifetime memory, though a situation you probably won't be experiencing. No two visits are alike, but no matter what the conditions, you are bound to have beautiful and fascinating moments on your visit here.

Prince Philip's Steps

The landing for this site is a dry one. The 25-meter (82-foot) trail up to the top of the cliff is steep and rocky, but there is a rustic handrailing to help you move along. The trail is in the cleft in the cliffs on the east side of Darwin Bay. The site was given its name after a visit by Great Britain's Prince Philip in 1964, when he did this rock scramble.

Once you reach level ground, at first you will be in a mix of low bush and open, gravelly spaces. There is a wealth of varied birdlife. One of the first species you may see is the red-footed booby, which nests on the low bushes here. After seeing blue-footed and Nazca boobies nesting on the ground, it seems incongruous to see their tree-borne counterparts perched above you, their garish red webbed feet curled over the branches they sit on. Do notice the pale blue "claws" extending from the red webbed feet. About 95 percent of the red-foot adults are a buffy brown; the other 5 percent are white. Both plumage types are the same species. The eyelids and long, hook-tipped beak are pale blue, with small patches of pink around the eyes.

Scattered over the island are nests of the Nazca booby, which uses several kinds of terrain for nesting. In general, their breeding season lasts from September to July. They have elaborate and almost bizarre territorial, mate selection, and nest maintenance displays, rivaling those of their blue- and red-footed relatives. Swallow-tailed gulls nest here also, right

LEFT: *Gripping nails of a red-footed booby* RIGHT: *Walking up Prince Philip's Steps, Genovesa*

in the open areas, in contrast to other nesting sites where they settle on rocky cliffs. Their babies are extremely well camouflaged, and it is fascinating to see how well they blend into the gray, gravelly surface of the open areas.

The scrubby flatlands also are the home of four finch species. The large ground finch of Genovesa is distinctive for having the heaviest bill of any of its species (the same species can show marked differences in some cases, depending on which island or islands it inhabits). The other finches are the sharp-beaked ground finch, the large cactus finch, and the warbler finch.

Among these birds can be found the Galapagos dove and the Genovesa subspecies of the Galapagos mockingbird (*Mimus parvulus bauri*), the smallest of this particular species. There may be nesting great

frigate birds established in the tops of the shrubs and small trees, as well, depending on the season. A few of the magnificent frigates nest on the island, too.

After you pass through the scrub brush, the trail comes out to the edge of a large lava field that stretches out before you to the sea. Visitors don't go onto that lava field, but there is an excellent view from the trail, which is higher up. At first it will look as if there is nothing to see, but then you will notice a small creature fluttering low over the lava, and then another. Suddenly you realize that you're seeing the constant movement of hundreds and even thousands of tiny storm petrels circling and twisting in flight. You also may spot thousands more offshore, like clouds of avian mosquitoes. Both the Galapagos storm petrel (*Oceanodroma tethys*) and the

Galapagos dove, Genovesa

band-rumped storm petrel (*Oceanodroma castro*) nest in crannies and tunnels beneath the rugged lava field surface.

From the low crest of ground where you stand to see the lava field, there are deep and narrow cracks in the earth harboring one of the major predators of the petrel, particularly the young ones: the short-eared owl (*Asio flammeus*). It is unusual in that it hunts day or night, but when I saw one it was just sitting quietly at the lip of one of the cracks, just a few meters away.

Finally, from your crest vantage point, the view of birds flying along the cliffs can be very rewarding. Red-billed tropicbirds, blue-footed boobies flying in platoons, Galapagos shearwaters (*Puffinus subalaris*), and noddy terns (*Anous stolidus*) all can be seen, complemented by frigate birds and perhaps red-footed and Nazca boobies returning from faraway fishing sorties.

11

SAN CRISTÓBAL

San Cristóbal is in the southeast quadrant of the Galapagos Islands. The island is becoming a major tourism site now that its airport is being used as the arrival or departure point for many visitors. San Cristóbal is the second most populated island in the Galapagos, and the government administrative center for the islands. There is an active farming industry, along with some fishing, and tourism is becoming a major sector.

San Cristóbal has had a long, not always pleasant human history. It had no regular inhabitants when Darwin visited San Cristóbal for five weeks in September 1835, his first landing in the islands. His first view of it (not at the comfortable harbor where you will disembark) was intimidating:

> Nothing could be less inviting than the first appearance. A broken field of black, basaltic lava, thrown into the most rugged waves, and crossed by

great fissures, is everywhere covered by stunted, sunburnt brushwood, which shows little signs of life. The dry and parched surface, being heated by the noonday sun, gave to the air a close and sultry feeling, like that from a stove; we fancied even that the bushes smelt unpleasantly.

What saved this particular excursion for Darwin was meeting two of the tortoises, something contemporary visitors will also likely experience. He reported,

> The day was glowing hot, and the scramble over the rough surface and through the intricate thickets, was very fatiguing; but I was well repaid by the strange Cyclopean scene. As I was walking along I met two large tortoises, each of which must have weighed two hundred pounds: one was eating a piece of cactus, and as I approached, it stared at me and slowly stalked away;

the other gave a deep hiss, and drew in its head. These huge reptiles, surrounded by the black lava, the leafless shrubs, and large cacti, seemed to my fancy like some antediluvian animals.

In 1841 a small settlement was established on San Cristóbal by a group of convicts who rebelled from their brutal treatment in the penal colony on Floreana Island. The sagas of the exploitation of convicts or laborers, and of repeated attempts to set up some form of island haven, continued into the twentieth century. The more recent human history is quite different, as the inhabitants increasingly adapt to—and create—a contemporary way of life.

One of the most striking examples of human adaptation and of sustainability in the Galapagos and in San Cristóbal in particular is the presence of a three-turbine wind-generation "farm" in the highlands. Its purpose is to reduce and eventually eliminate the reliance on diesel fuel for producing electricity. Less diesel usage would also reduce risks of fuel spills, which Galapagos has experienced, to its sorrow, with one boat running aground as recently as January 2015. The wind-generation project requires the collaboration of residents, local authorities, the Park Service, the Ecuadorean national government, and a number of international funders and contributors of expertise, equipment, and the actual wind turbines themselves. There have been glitches now and then—the occasional

equipment breakdowns, for example, and also the wind has not always been as consistently strong as is needed for maximum production.

However, as of October 1, 2013, the San Cristóbal Wind Project completed six years of operation. During these six years, it has delivered 18,309 megawatt-hours to San Cristóbal, or 31 percent of the total island power consumption. This means that the project has saved the use of about 6 million liters (1.6 million gallons) of diesel fuel and prevented the addition of fifteen thousand tons of carbon monoxide into the atmosphere. The project has won international awards for sustainability.

Directly south of San Cristóbal is Española Island (see chapter 13), and to the west Floreana (see chapter 12).

PUERTO BAQUERIZO MORENO

The port community of San Cristóbal, Puerto Baquerizo Moreno, has a population of about fifty-five hundred. A ramble down the main street is very interesting. There is a huge "public art" mural perfect for trip log pictures, many cafes, and a number of local offices offering a range of activities—trips to the lush highlands, to the Tortoise Reserve, to trails and hiking, surfing, snorkeling, scuba diving.

The waterfront street is the very attractive Charles Darwin Malecón (waterfront walkway). The community has enclosed a small segment of the shoreline, creating a pool that at high tide is a swimming pool,

Local dive shop, San Cristóbal

with a modest waterslide. Whatever the water level, there are sea lions, especially younger ones, playing in the protected area. It is also a great place to see both herons and Sally Lightfoot crabs searching for food. Shorebirds also come there, and are easily seen and photographed. As you walk farther along, there is a kind of boat graveyard, where old fishing boats or other vessels are locked into the sand, tipped onto their sides, quietly rotting.

There are benches here and there along the Malecón, providing comfortable places to sit and absorb the sights and sounds of this busy port.

Puerto Baquerizo Moreno also is the jumping-off point for several day trips to nearby islands, including Isla Lobos and Kicker Rock, both impressive sites. Isla Lobos offers a dry landing, sea lions, and frigate birds. Kicker Rock (León Dormido, "sleeping lion" in Spanish) is observed from your panga—there is not a landing there. Isla Lobos is a brief land visit. These sites are often visited on the last afternoon before the departure from the airport just outside of the town.

THE INTERPRETATION CENTER

This center, inaugurated in August 1998, is a spectacular addition to the island. Its supporters included the Spanish government and the government of Ecuador. The center is on the edge of Puerto Baquerizo Moreno, and can be reached by a short bus ride, arranged by your

Interpretation Center, San Cristóbal

guide, or by taking a 15-minute walk from the town center.

The center is wonderfully designed to tell the natural and human history of the islands and to serve as an active educational resource for visitors along with island school-children and other residents. It is a beautiful, light, airy building, made of the local stone and wood to blend into the slightly hilly landscape on which it is located. You move easily from room to room, from era to era of archipelago history. The displays are stunning, with their portrayals of the geological evolution of the islands and colorful displays of land and marine life.

The human history is told through a combination of paintings, old photographs, and three-dimensional recreations of early life on the islands. The horrendous story of the penal colony that existed for more than 150 years, until it was closed in 1959 when the appalling conditions there became known internationally, is riveting and dismaying at the same time. Equally well told is the intriguing story of some of the twentieth century's distinctive immigrants from Europe, with broken dreams, divided loyalties, and suspected murders.

For a little break from the learning, take a few minutes to walk outside the building along the boardwalks that extend into the surrounding thickets of palo santo trees and other dry, lowland vegetation. The wind sweeps up the hillside from the harbor, and you will have excellent views of the water a kilometer or so away.

CERRO COLORADO TORTOISE RESERVE AND REARING CENTER

The Cerro Colorado Tortoise Reserve and Rearing Center was established in 2004. Located in the higher, moist area of the southeastern part of San Cristóbal,

it is 22 kilometers (13.7 miles) from the port, and is reached by a 40-minute bus or taxi ride. It is a Park Service visitor site, and you must be accompanied by a guide.

The center was established because of the precarious state of the San Cristóbal tortoise (*Chelonoidis chathamensis*), threatened by the population of cats, rats, and goats, which have yet to have been eradicated. Just as with the captive rearing program in Puerto Ayora, eggs are collected from nests in the wild, and taken in for incubating and hatching, then placed in growing pens and fed their natural food. When they are big enough to survive in the wild, they are returned to their home territory.

The Cerro Colorado area is one of the few places where it is possible to see the

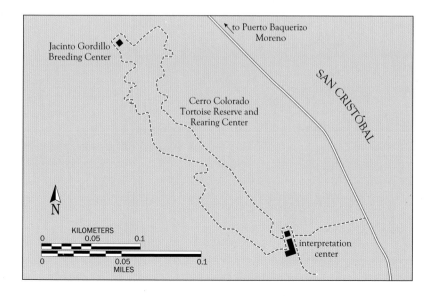

endemic plant *Calandrinia galapagosa*, which is in danger of extinction because of the goats. The flower is small, white and pink open-faced, with five petals. The Park Service now has a cultivation program for the plant, raising numbers of them in greenhouses, to preserve this heritage and to be ready to reestablish them in the wild, once the goats are eradicated.

EL JUNCO LAGOON

This whole round-trip is an easy one and takes only two to three hours, depending on how much time you spend enjoying the birding and the view. This small freshwater lake is located at about 700 meters (2300 feet) in elevation. It is one of the few lakes in the islands that does not go dry periodically, though its levels can vary as much as 5 meters (16.5 feet), depending on whether it is the rainy season or not, or how heavy the rain is. The lake and its shores are an excellent place for birding, and the trip up to it takes you through several vegetation zones. You reach the lake by bus or taxi, arranging this on your own, or it may be a part of a day-tour or part of your longer live-aboard boat trip. As you move along, you will be passing into the more humid levels of the island, where there are farms.

The view of the lagoon itself is lovely, and the birding is a wonderful mixture of shorebirds, drawn by the fresh water, and the island's distinctive land birds. The lake attracts whimbrels, stilts, white-cheeked pintail ducks, and common gallinules. Even though this is quite far inland, the oceangoing frigate birds are often seen bathing in the fresh water. As for land birds, seven of the Darwin's finches are listed as being here. Telling one from another is a challenge. You might be particularly lucky and see a warbler finch here, with its tiny thin bill. It's hard to believe it is actually a finch.

12

FLOREANA

Floreana is located west of Española at the southern edge of the archipelago, almost exactly at the east–west center. The island is about a three- to five-hour boat trip from the south coast of Santa Cruz or from Española.

Floreana has the smallest number of people of the four communities in the Galapagos, with some 150 residents, most living in the village of Puerto Velasco Ibarra. There are several places to stay there. The hotel on Black Beach was established by one of the European families who came here in the 1930s looking for a life of total self-sufficiency and some form of paradise. Their descendants still operate their hotel.

Floreana is in the process of developing sustainable business alternatives for local residents. This focuses on tourism, but given its holistic approach, the work includes learning how best to manage scarce water, energy, and food resources. This collaborative community effort is based on principles of eco-tourism, a commitment both to conserve the natural environment and promote sustainable living for residents. This includes the active engagement of residents in protecting and restoring their island home.

Floreana is the only island with a year-round supply of water (from a spring). This resource is closely linked to the island's dramatic and mysterious human history, starting with pirates and buccaneers making it a regular stopover. The European arrivals of the 1930s have been the source of much conjecture, conflicting viewpoints, and a great deal of research—some credible and some questionable. There were unexplained deaths, overlapping relationships, feuds, and plenty of plain hard work of trying to wrest a living out of the harsh environment. Your guide can tell you stories, and a web search will yield substantial amounts of information and anecdote. A team of well-respected documentary filmmakers spent more

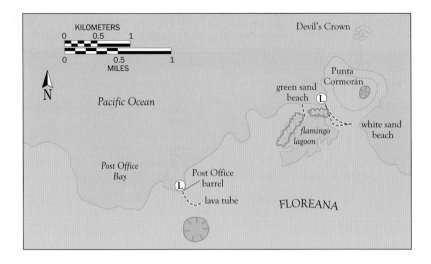

than ten years developing the story of the early settlers, their dreams, lives, deaths, and continued presence through the following generations on Floreana. The film (*The Galapagos Affair: Satan Came to Eden*) has enjoyed success on the film festival circuit since its release in 2014.

There are four visitor land sites on Floreana: Punta Cormorán, with its lagoon and two lovely beaches; Post Office Bay, still the place to send mail to friends around the world; a lava tube that can be followed far underground; and Asilo de la Paz, the site of the freshwater spring.

Just northwest of Punta Cormorán is Devil's Crown, an excellent diving site just a few hundred meters (around a thousand feet) off Floreana, usually reached from the Punta Cormorán anchorage. This partially submerged lava cone provides a protected area for swimming and

snorkeling. If the weather is good and the sea calm, you'll want to get into your panga for the short trip to the middle of the Crown and slip over the side for a few minutes of underwater photography.

PUNTA CORMORÁN

Punta Cormorán is a steep, small lava cone on a point of land joined to the larger island by a low-lying strip of vegetated dune. You approach the site by a wet landing in a pleasant cove. The beach sand itself is of interest because it has a large proportion of olivine crystals, derived from volcanic action, which have a pale green color.

You move up the usual beach slope, passing through the dune vegetation. Shortly, the trail ascends slightly along a hill that faces the cone itself. At the high point of the trail, only a few minutes from the start, you look down into a large lagoon. Its water level varies greatly, from mostly mudflats to nearly a lake in an El Niño year. At any time, it is likely to be an excellent place for bird-watching. Flamingos are common. From this height you can see the underwater trails they make through the mud as they sieve through the turbid water to extract minute crustaceans. At first you may think the lines are the traces of cracks that were formed in the mud when it was very dry, but then as you follow a flamingo's movements you see that these curving, wobbling lines are made by their feet shuffling through the mud.

The edges of the lagoon, particularly on the northwest side, have vegetation right to the water and are good for spotting shorebirds. We saw a phalarope (no one could decide which species), a willet, and white-cheeked pintail ducks. Whimbrels,

semipalmated plovers, ruddy turnstones, and wandering tattlers are regularly seen there in small numbers, too. Don't forget to look at the birdlife right around you at the viewpoint. Galapagos large-billed flycatchers can be very evident, and they seem to like to perch staring at visitors, making them surprisingly easy to photograph. There are a variety of the finches, and your guide may be able to help you sort them out for those working on their birding life list.

After you pause at the viewpoint, you will go about 350 meters (1150 feet) farther to one of the best beaches in the islands. Lining a shallow cove with white sand as fine as granulated sugar, the beach is the home of multitudes of ghost crabs. They hide from your approach and then come up from their tiny holes to skitter down the beach in search of food. You

LEFT: *Ghost crab tracks* RIGHT: *Ghost crab, Floreana*

can see the little globs of sand they leave as they move along, but you'll be lucky to actually see them because of their shyness and the difficulty of picking out their pale, translucent bodies in the bright sand, even when they are aboveground.

Once when we were at this beach, it was visited by a number of stingrays, which were about a meter across. They came right up to the shoreline, just skimming along well within view.

Swimming and snorkeling are excellent here. The beach falls away gradually, and there were no waves or currents. It is just right for gently stroking from one side of the cove to the other or for standing quietly in the water and watching the light change on the palo santo trees that clothe Floreana's graceful slopes.

POST OFFICE BAY

If you want to feel as if you are part of human history, Post Office Bay is the place to go. Darwin came to this spot, and you'll see mementos of many more recent visitors.

Post Office Bay is just a short boat ride to the west of Punta Cormorán. You land on a brown beach, perhaps sharing it with a few sea lions, and walk beyond the beach a couple of minutes to a small clearing in the scrub.

It is rather exciting to discover that a process for communication around the world still exists here, centered on a wooden barrel, with a hinged door in the middle of its side. Barrels such as these

were once commonly used across the Pacific for sailors to communicate. They would drop letters off into the barrel and pick up any addressed to a location they expected to go on their voyage, and deliver it themselves. Floreana's system was first recorded in a whaling ship's records from 1793, and it is the only process of its kind still in use around the world.

For today's visitor, the guide pulls the letters from the barrel and you pick out any addressed to someone near enough to your hometown that you can deliver it personally. (Or if that's not possible, you can mail it from home, maybe attaching a note about when you picked it up.) You can leave a letter in the barrel as well. The ones that we had deposited were delivered before we got home ourselves, so it can be a pretty effective process. That is the tradition, and visitors maintain it.

Because of the heavy use of this most interesting process, the Park Service has over time recreated new sturdier barrels, and there is even a kind of "roof" over the current one to protect it from the elements. It is quite a different experience from when as late as 2010 visitors were met with a decrepit, if fascinating, whitewashed old barrel, with pieces of board with the names of visiting ships—including tour boats—leaning on the supporting post or even piled around the base of the post. It was fun, almost like historic graffiti, but that approach is no longer in keeping with contemporary eco-tourism principles. The barrel is still a barrel, but the area is less "informal," though still providing an opportunity to carry on a vital tradition.

As you walk around this area, having taken care of your postal activities, you can see the remains of a small Norwegian settlement's effort to install a fish cannery in the 1920s. There are a couple of large, rusting containers, with some writing on them, but the people have long gone.

THE LAVA TUBE

This lava tube starts out as a hole in the flat ground about 10 minutes' walk past the Post Office barrel. A wooden staircase descends 5 meters (16.5 feet) or so to the first level spot, with a low-ceilinged shaft down to the floor. You will walk a few minutes along the smooth bottom until you encounter water. Visitors who want to continue then tend to take off their shoes and continue through the deepening water, walking and even half-swimming to reach the end of the cave—and return the same way. If you do intend to go to the end of the tube, you will need a flashlight. This whole excursion to the end of the tube and back takes about an hour.

ASILO DE LA PAZ

You can visit Asilo de la Paz, the site of the freshwater spring, by walking from Puerto Velasco Ibarra, but you have to calculate that it's 8 kilometers (5 miles) on foot following the municipal road. You can also hire a bus to go up in 45 minutes and then walk about 350 meters (1150 feet) until you reach the spring. This is not a

Heading down into a lava tube, Floreana

part of the national park, as such, but it is often a part of the guided tours—or you may go there on your own.

This is a very historic and beautiful area in the highlands of Floreana. At the high point of your hike in, there is a panoramic view of the highlands and then the gentle slopes to the sea. Asilo de la Paz is the place where drinking water has always been available. Pirates discovered this fact hundreds of years ago; how they did so, considering that the location is rather far from the little harbor of Puerto Valasco Ibarra, is amazing, but somehow it happened. The settlers from the early 1930s also relied on this water, and even as late as 1980 people still came to collect it in plastic containers. However, now there is a pipe that supplies water to the community, installed by volunteers from the community working together as a "Minga," or cooperative effort.

As you hike or are driven up to this area, you can see the different vegetation zones. In general, as altitude increases, so does moisture, and then the plant life is more lush. However, there is a variation in the plant life of these eco-zones due to farming and ranching in the nonpark areas, and thus there is a mix of bush and pasturage or farmed field, along with the original vegetation. You'll also see some of the homes of people who live on the island, with children waving at you as you go by.

The other historic site you will see on this visit is the pirate caves. These are the smallest caves for human habitation that one could imagine, little more than two or three vertical indentations in a few cliff faces, perhaps hollowed out further by hand. Surely no more than two or three hardy, begrimed souls at any one time could have found shelter here. There are still the smudges of fires from yesteryear, but it is hard to fathom that anyone could make this even a temporary home. The whole place makes you keenly aware of water as a life-giving, life-saving element.

After your visit to the water source and the pirate caves, you probably will go on a little tour of the more open land surrounding the area. The birding there is excellent, and it is one of your chances to see the medium tree finch.

Though the Asilo site is not within park boundaries, and is part of the agricultural zone of the islands, the Park Service has established a very large corral for some thirty tortoises that were once kept by locals as pets. Here you can wander at leisure and get close to the tortoises for photographs.

DEVIL'S CROWN

Devil's Crown is a small but very exciting place to visit. It is located just 250 meters (820 feet) from Floreana's shore, a few minutes' panga ride from the Punta Cormorán anchorage. Devil's Crown is the partially exposed cone of an extinct volcano. Its once-complete circle of rock has been broken in several places, allowing the sea to come in. Its black sides are so steep, craggy, and harsh-looking that it's easy to see how it could acquire this sinister name.

As you can see from your boat, or via a panga ride around the Crown, its craggy walls are splashed at the top with the whitewash of bird excrement, and the only thing that seems to grow there are two kinds of cactus, the candelabra cactus (*Jasminocereus thouarsii*) and the prickly pear (*Opuntia megasperma*). Birds love the place, and you can see red-billed tropicbirds, pelicans, lava gulls, and frigate birds sitting on the jagged rocks, loafing or waiting for the right time to go out to feed. Even the occasional heron can be seen there.

Snorkeling and scuba diving are very popular here. If you get a chance to do either, you will be very glad you did. For scuba diving you will need to be on a day-trip or live-aboard tour that is specifically for divers. Snorkeling is usually a part of day trips or tours that have snorkeling as one of the activity options, often supplying you with the basic gear for swimming from the panga. If you are not a confident swimmer, be sure to talk with your guide about whether snorkeling is for you. The currents around the Crown are fierce and the water can be cold, so you'll want to make the decision that is best for you.

It is also likely that there will be an option of traveling around the Crown in the panga, viewing the occasional penguin on the rocks or peering into the water, looking for sharks or other large marine life. The marine life is dreamlike in its beauty and variety. From huge sea lions whipping past you, to penguins swimming nearby, to layer upon layer of different fish species as well as sea stars, tube corals, and sea cucumbers on the bottom, you are bound to be impressed and delighted.

This is definitely the place where an underwater camera is invaluable. Some very inexpensive ones these days are perfectly adequate for taking excellent pictures. On my latest trip one of the travelers had just happened to pick one up in Quito, just a little underwater "point-and-shoot," and the results were wonderful.

13

ESPAÑOLA

Española (Hood) Island is the nesting site of the waved albatross, and there are colonies of Nazca and blue-footed boobies. When you land on Española, you are greeted by some of the largest and most colorful of the marine iguanas. Their bodies often have swaths of red and green colors mixed in with the usual dark gray or black. There are usually lots of sea lions around as well.

Española is a fairly flat island, rising slightly from sea level on its north side to rugged black cliffs perhaps 30 meters (100 feet) high on its south side. There are two visitor sites here: the long white beach at Gardner Bay, home of sea lions and shorebirds; and the tilted plateau of Punta Suarez, breeding area of the waved albatross and two species of booby.

PUNTA SUAREZ

The landing at Punta Suarez is one of the more exciting you will have, because the boat has to anchor about 200 meters

(a tenth of a mile) or more out to sea. Depending on the tides, the panga must take a circuitous route over barely submerged rocks, through daunting waves, to get to the sheltered calm of its landing place. Extra caution with cameras is called for here; keep them well protected.

Once you land, you are immediately in the midst of such numbers and variety of wildlife that it is almost too much to absorb. An endemic Española mockingbird will be likely there to greet you as you arrive. There are usually many sea lions, both in the little cove and right on shore where you disembark. Then within a few steps you see dozens of marine iguanas on the rocks at the back edge of the sandy beach.

These iguanas are not like any others in the islands. They are the same species, but the Española race is very distinct for its striking coloring. It has patches of dark red on its sides, a greenish tinge along its ridged back, and the usual black everywhere else.

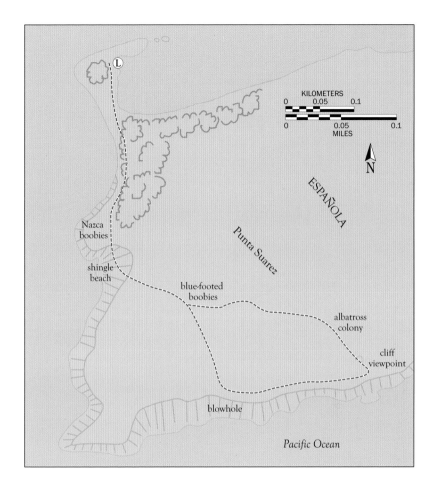

If you see lava lizards, these are a species unique to Española (Microlophus delanonis). These are the largest lava lizards in the islands; they are also notable for having the shortest, thickest tail. The female has red under her chin and at the base of her tail. The male is speckled black, yellow, and green.

If you are here between November and June, you will be there during the nesting period for Nazca boobies. You come upon their nesting area within just a few more steps as you reach the first approach to a cliff edge. They have a yearly breeding cycle, starting in November with egg laying and ending in June when the young

Nazca booby catching the breeze, Española

are able to fly and feed on their own. Next you will descend for a few meters to a small shingle beach and then go back up to the open expanses of low scrub and open areas that cover the island.

Your next treat is a large nesting area for blue-footed boobies. They do not have the distinctively defined breeding season of the Nazca boobies, and you may see eggs or any stage of development in the young at any time of year.

Beautiful Galapagos doves will be pecking and probing on the ground here and there. They seem less wary of people here than they are on other islands. Completely unwary and actually very assertive and outgoing is the endemic Española mockingbird (*Mimus macdonaldi,* still generally known as the "Hood" species), which is found only here and on a nearby rocky islet, Gardner-near-Hood. It is somewhat larger than the other three endemic mockingbird species, with a heavier, more down-curved beak. It has hazel-colored eyes, which you could possibly be close enough to see because these mockers are nearly pestiferous in their approach to people. They hop on your shoes, sit on your hat, and jump on your day pack. You can get some personalized pictures without engaging in inappropriate behavior to lure them to you. They come whether you encourage it or not.

Scan the bushes for the large-billed subspecies of the large cactus finch (*Geospiza conirostris*) and a very gray warbler finch subspecies (*Certhidea olivacea*). The small ground finch (*Geospiza fuliginosa*) nests here, and so does the large-billed flycatcher.

Then, just about 400 meters (0.25 mile) from the beginning of the trail, you will come to the only place where the waved albatross nests (with the exception of a few pairs that nest on a tiny island off the coast of Ecuador). The eggs are laid between April and June, and then the parents incubate them for two months. Once hatched, the fledglings need until sometime in December to be ready to fly. The approximately twelve thousand pairs that nest yearly on Española are, effectively, the entire population of this bird in the world. For the nature lover there is something very moving about being within a few meters of all the varied activity that goes on as these birds lay their eggs and care for their young.

The setting is quite dramatic, for you are near the edge of high, black cliffs, with the waves far below rolling in from the open sea to the east. Many kinds of seabirds sit next to you on the rocks, and others soar above and below you. And every few minutes, especially in the early

morning, a huge albatross waddles to the edge of the cliff, makes a few awkward wing flaps, and then launches itself out on the updrafts to become one of the world's most graceful and efficient soaring beings.

Depending on when you are there, you may see a great deal of the elaborate display these birds make as they claim and maintain territory or as they form pairs and trade off the care of their young at the nest. They mate for life, so only birds mating for their first time, at four or five years of age, will be doing the

Mockingbird that is endemic to Española

pair-formation or courtship displays to any great degree. However, toward the end of the breeding season, already established pairs will do displays like this as they consolidate their relationship for the year to come.

There are several detailed descriptions of the displays in the scientific literature, but to the uninitiated, the central theme of the courtship movement seems to be variations on fencing. The birds cross bills, click them, throw their heads high, make loud honking noises, and then resume the thrust and dodge of their bills. It's noisy and exciting to watch. Part of the display is a vast exaggeration of their

ordinary rolling walk, a gait that makes them look like the most drunken sailor just hitting dry land after months in a very small boat at sea.

If you are fortunate enough to be here during the breeding season, being able to see the huge eggs, the downy ugly chicks, the fledglings trying out their wings, and the waddling adults transforming themselves into incomparably fine flyers, you will be experiencing one of the premier privileges of visiting the Galapagos.

On the way back from the albatross grounds, the trail traces the cliff edges and you will have an excellent view of the blowhole that shoots a plume of spray 15

The island's blowhole at high tide, Española

Swallow-tailed gull preening, Española

to 30 meters (50 to 100 feet) in the air. There is a crevice at sea level where the surging water rushes in and is then almost trapped except for this one upward exit. The spume is impressive to watch, but safety considerations mean you'll simply be enjoying the sight from above and probably taking a lot of pictures.

Keep your binoculars ready for viewing along the shoreline, because the area is a good one for seeing shorebirds such as the oystercatcher, a few of which breed on Española. The rocky cliffs are nesting places for the swallow-tailed gull, the red-billed tropicbird, and Audubon's shearwater.

If you are really lucky, you may even see a giant tortoise. Around two thousand have been returned from the Park Service captive rearing program and have been breeding in the wild since the 1990s. Although goats were eliminated from Española in 1978, their ongoing impact is evident in major changes to the plant community, that is, woody plants have been able to flourish and spread. In so doing they impede the spread of the *Opuntia* cactus, the primary food of the tortoises, and they also make it harder for the tortoises to wander around and get to the cactus. This changed vegetation situation has thus created another kind of imbalance in the ecological structure of the island, resulting in loss of tortoise and albatross habitat and placing a constraint upon successful reproduction. The situation is being carefully monitored by the Park Service and is the subject of some major environmental research by local and international scientists. The complexity of the food web, the roles and relationships of plants and animals, is a constant source of fascination and concern.

GARDNER BAY

This dazzlingly white shoreline of slightly more than a kilometer (about a half mile) is an "open area," where visitors can wander freely. However, there are sea turtle nests in the low bushes at the upper edges of the shore, so visitors must be careful not to walk near there; your guide will point this out. The beach is also a breeding area for

sea lions, which form a kind of brown, furry line along the sand, parallel to the waterline but a few yards up. Here again you will want to be cautious and avoid getting too close to the males (larger, rather high foreheads, and sometimes an aggressive manner). This caution includes not getting between males and females or intruding between any adults and young ones.

There are often migrating and resident shorebirds here. I've seen whimbrels on nearly every visit, and last time there was a wandering tattler. The strikingly colored oystercatcher can be seen, sometimes wading in the shallow water, or preening on the shore, or even sitting and resting in the sunshine.

There are a number of rocky islets close to the shore. They aren't for visiting, but they make the view even more interesting. Watch for birds or sea lions spending some time there.

Sun, sand, and sea lions in a perfect formation, Española

14

ISABELA

I sabela and Fernandina are the westernmost of the islands of the archipelago. Isabela, the largest and longest of the islands, extends in a north–south direction, and Fernandina is located on the western side of Isabela. Visitation options for Isabela include the live-aboard four- or eight-day tours—make sure beforehand that the islands are on your itinerary—or island-hopping and staying for several days in local accommodations and then doing day trips for hiking, snorkeling, surfing, or scuba diving. These activities are based from the small community of Puerto Villamil, on the southeast coast of Isabela. It has a number of hotels of varying levels of service and amenities, many cafes, and lots of services offering touring options.

Isabela has the most imposing terrain in the islands, composed as it is of six towering shield volcanoes that have merged over the millennia, forming the mountainous profile seen today. All of

the volcanoes except Ecuador are still active. Two of the six volcanoes, Wolf and Cerro Azul, are more than 1700 meters (about 1 mile) high. Alcedo, located at the north–south midpoint of the island, is about 1200 meters (4000 feet) high. The youngest volcano is Cerro Azul, followed by Wolf, Darwin, Alcedo, and Sierra Negra. This whole area, including nearby Fernandina Island, is extremely active, having recorded several volcanic eruptions in the past few decades, most recently Wolf in 2015. Notably, the Sierra Negra caldera is 10 kilometers (6.2 miles) across and is the second largest in the world (the largest is Ngorongoro Crater in Tanzania).

There are several Park Service visitor sites on Isabela, including the visitor center at the Arnaldo Tupiza Tortoise Breeding Center, Tagus Cove, Urbina Bay, and Las Tintoreras. The walk up Sierra Negra volcano is a main attraction for visitors, too. There are many other activities and places to visit for those who can stay a few days in Villamil and do day trips.

ARNALDO TUPIZA TORTOISE BREEDING CENTER

The Arnaldo Tupiza Tortoise Breeding Center is designated by the Park Service as an educational site, where visitors can see the captive rearing of giant tortoises from southern Isabela. Since the 1990s, they have been collected from the slopes of the Sierra Negra volcano, and from a number of volcanic cones in the area. Rescue and captive breeding have been essential to counter the threats of fire, volcanic eruptions, and predation by rats, competition for food from feral goats, as well as the trampling of nests by feral donkeys, and the negative impacts of hunting by humans.

The center is 1.5 kilometers (about 1 mile) outside of Puerto Villamil, just a walk or short taxi ride. There is interpretive information about the history and activities of the captive rearing program. The tortoises are carefully studied to determine their genetic makeup, and to trace their original distribution over southern Isabela. Visitors have a good view of the tortoises lumbering along as they wander from place to place in the compounds, chomping away at their food, at their own measured pace. The center also has its own native garden of endemic plants—an excellent learning opportunity.

LAS TINTORERAS

This is an islet just a 10-minute panga ride from town. The trail follows the perimeter of the islet. Except for a segment of white sand beach and another of black stone, most of the trail is on *a-a* lava (a gritty type described in chapter 8's section "Sulivan Bay Lava Flows"), so wear protective footgear. The black stone beach is lined with button mangrove (*Conocarpus erecta*) and white mangrove (*Laguncularia racemosas*). The water is calm and crystal clear, and the animal life is rich—sea lions, birds, nesting marine iguanas, reef sharks, sea turtles, rays. Swimming is not allowed here, because the many pools and the calm water create a perfect daytime resting place for a number of marine species that are nocturnal. You can see the marine life from many vantage points, though, so be sure you have your polarizing filter for your camera.

TAGUS COVE

Tagus Cove is on the northwest side of Isabela. It is only reachable via live-aboard boats. There are two activities for the visitor, one on land and the other on water. The land trip is a 1.8-kilometer (1.1-mile) walk up to Darwin Lake, a saltwater lagoon that is actually above sea level. The slopes are clothed with typical arid zone vegetation. This walk is very appealing for its good selection of birds, fine view of a crater lake, and views of Darwin and Wolf volcanoes.

Tagus Cove is a breeding area for the flightless cormorant. These birds nest near the shore, where they can readily get to the water, which is where they come into their own. It is a real privilege to be able to see these distinctive birds—reflecting the diversity of evolutionary adaptations in far-flung locations, such as the Galapagos Islands, and how in the absence of predators, birds can lose the capacity of flight. When you are on the trail, you will probably see a variety of finches (possibly even the woodpecker finch), mockingbirds, and even evidence of tortoises, if not the beasts themselves. This also is often a great area for seeing the Galapagos hawk.

The cliffs that enfold the bay are marred by extensive graffiti, put there by crews and passengers of many of the ships that have come here over the years. The ones that are very old have some historical interest from days when few traveled to remote places, but fortunately this

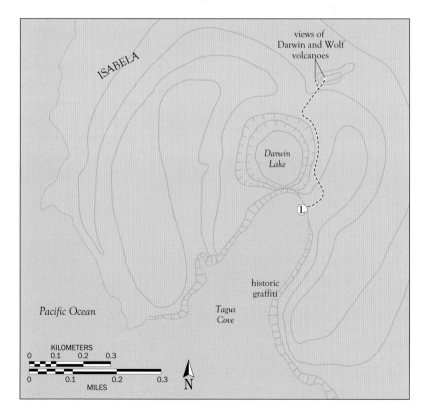

Lagoon in a lava field, Isabela

practice has been sufficiently discouraged that it has become almost extinct in modern times.

The other activity for visitors is a ride in the panga along the cliffs. Near the entrance of the cove are shelves of rock, and here you may see a few Galapagos penguins and flightless cormorants. Blue-footed boobies are common, and there may be marine iguanas. The panga ride is a very pleasant way to see the sea-based wildlife from another perspective, although it can be difficult to photograph from the gently rocking boat.

URBINA BAY

Urbina Bay is also on the west coast of Isabela, at the western base of Alcedo volcano. It is reachable only by a live-aboard boat with its licensed guide. There is a wet landing, and if the seas are high, you may not be able to land—the beach is steep and surf can be heavy.

Once on land, the trail is 3.2 kilometers (2 miles) long, starting along the shore and then moving into the scrubland at somewhat higher level. As you progress along the trail, you come to what looks like just another scrubby plain stretching out beyond. But this area is extremely interesting because it has a dramatic and beautiful example of the geological activity of the islands. In 1954, 5 kilometers (3.1 miles) of the marine reef at the edge of the shore were uplifted 4 meters (13 feet).

No one was there at the time, but not too long afterward a film crew was sailing in the area and they noticed that the beach area gleamed unusually white. As they got closer, they saw that this whiteness was caused by conglomerates of coral and calcium-based algae that were out of their watery element. On these uplifted

rocks were stranded sea animals—lobsters, marine turtles, and even fish—in the pools in the pitted surface. Obviously, if these active animals had been trapped like that, the whole event must have happened very recently and very quickly.

Exactly why it happened is not clear, but the likelihood is that some subterranean shift of molten lava, perhaps caused by volcanic activity on Alcedo or the more southern Sierra Negra volcano, was responsible for this movement of Earth's crust.

Walking on dry land right in the middle of a bed of coral, with large boulders of it

Coral uplifted from the sea, Isabela

that can be head-high can be an odd sensation. The globular coral, curiously brainlike in surface texture, is now dull black. The clumps of coral with their intricate surfaces, and the remnants of barnacles, seashells, sea worms, and other creatures embedded in them or strewn about make for a beautiful place. Because coral quickly dries out and deteriorates easily, be careful not to disturb it.

There is snorkeling in the bay, and it is an excellent place to see the spiny lobster (*Panulirus pencillatus*) and the green lobster (*Panulirus gracilis*).

OTHER OPTIONS ON ISABELA

Given Isabela's size and diverse environment, and the ready access to a number of sites and activities for the visitor who wants to arrange their own adventures from Puerto Villamil, it is worth noting a few of these opportunities here. These include horseback riding and hiking to Chico volcano on the slopes of Sierra Negra volcano; snorkeling at Los Túneles; Laguna Concha de Perla for swimming and snorkeling; visiting the Wall of Tears, the remains of the penal colony that closed in 1959; swimming at Playa del Amor: a small beach ending in a shallow intertidal lagoon, ideal for children; walking at low tide in the Túnel del Estero, a lava tube out to the sea; and seeing the largest black mangrove trees in Galapagos from the El Estero Trail.

15

FERNANDINA

Fernandina, the westernmost island, is one of the most volcanically active in the archipelago. Because of its distance from the center of the islands and because there is a particularly lengthy trip to reach it, Fernandina is less visited than the other main islands. It is an intriguing place and well worth the trip if it can be managed. Visitation here is only possible via fully-guided, live-aboard tour boats.

This island is about 1500 meters (about 1 mile) high, with its main crater about 6.5 kilometers (4 miles) wide. One of the newest islands geologically, it does not have the rich floral life that some of the other islands of its height display, partly because so much of it has been coated with recent lava flows and volcanic ash, and partly because Isabela's heights capture much of the rain it might get from moist air coming from the east.

Fernandina's La Cumbre volcano has erupted several times in the twentieth century. In 1968 it erupted and the floor of its crater, already 610 meters (2000 feet) below its rim, dropped another few hundred meters. In 1977 the volcano erupted again, sending rivers of lava into its lake from a crack in the crater wall. The next year another eruption occurred, with more lava spewed into the crater. The most spectacular eruption was in January 1995. Since then the volcano has erupted several more times, most recently in 2009. But unless you are here at one of those special explosive times, you will be seeing only the outside slopes of this crater, along with sweeps of black lava from flows that happened before our time.

The island is exceptional in having no introduced mammals—no cats, rats, goats. It is the home of large numbers of marine iguanas, which nest there from January to June. Also making their homes there are flightless cormorants, penguins, the Galapagos hawk, and the Galapagos snake. Fernandina is also the home of the mangrove finch, now being rescued

Resting marine iguanas, Fernandina

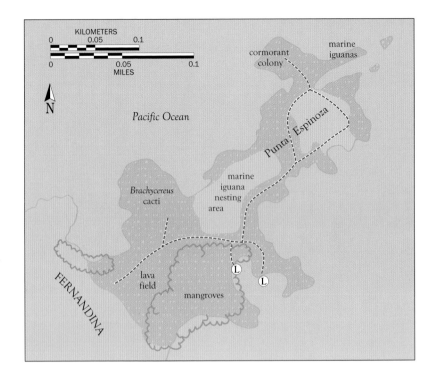

from the very brink of extinction (see the "Birds" section in chapter 3).

The only visitor site on Fernandina is Punta Espinoza.

PUNTA ESPINOZA

The landing area is dry and in a tiny, mangrove-lined inlet. The landing site is a spit of black lava rock, reminiscent of the recent flows of Sulivan Bay. Sometimes there are many marine iguanas right here, on the rocks. From the landing sites the trail goes in two directions, left to a field of harsh, sharp a-a lava and to the right to the "land's end."

The point itself has rich and varied wildlife, even if the surroundings are stark and might seem to be barren. But this is far from the case. Areas of mangrove bush provide a home for marine and terrestrial life, including nesting flightless cormorants and penguins. You may see a number of marine iguanas perched on the rocks or basking on bits of driftwood sticking out from the cracks in the lava. This is also a place where sea lion pups are seen in breeding season.

When you are quietly walking among the mangrove trees, keep your eye out for a variety of herons. Yellow warblers,

Marine iguana, Fernandina

Galapagos hawks, and mockingbirds are found here, too. Great blue herons and some pelicans nest here, and frigate birds settle into the mangrove bush as well.

The shore area is a good place to look for migrant shorebirds and for petrels, shearwaters, and frigate birds. The Galapagos shearwaters apparently fly inland at night to roost in the crevices of the broken lava fields.

Opposite: *Typical eco-lodge in the rain forest*

PART IV

MAINLAND ECUADOR—
AN ESSENTIAL PART
OF YOUR TRAVELS

I f you're planning to go as far as the Galapagos, take the time to visit mainland Ecuador, a magnificent country with extraordinarily varied geography, peoples, and natural and human history. These travel guidelines are based on a three-week trip overall, with the final week in the Galapagos and the first two weeks on the mainland, divided between time in Quito and the surrounding highlands, time spent in an eco-lodge in the rain forest, and a day or so along the coast. This is what I've done on my last ten trips, and it is what most travelers can afford to devote to a major trip.

These trips were guided tours, with groups no larger than six people. Even though there was a well-defined itinerary, there was a lot of flexibility in the day-to-day travel, with stops along the way to spot birds, or photograph a particular vista, or to walk up a hill or down a ravine, or to follow a crystal-clear stream.

Ecuador is a relatively small country, just 276,840 square kilometers (106,890 square miles), or about the size of the state of Nevada. It is a little more than 1000 kilometers (620 miles) from north to south, and the Pan-American Highway runs along its north–south axis, from the Colombian border, through Quito, and down to Guayaquil. The population of little more than 25 million is concentrated in urban areas. Guayaquil is Ecuador's largest city and its major port, with a population of more than three million. The capital, Quito, has just fewer than two million. The third largest city is Cuenca.

Ecuador has hundreds of volcanic mountain peaks, with nine being taller than 5000 meters (16,000 feet). The highest of all is Chimborazo, at 6310 meters (20,702 feet). Interestingly, because of the equatorial bulge, which gives Earth an elliptical form, the top of Chimborazo is the world's most distant point from the center of Earth, making it the world's highest mountain, if the baseline is Earth's center and not sea level. As with the Galapagos Islands, Ecuador's topography exhibits a range of altitudes, from the high Andes and dipping down to a few hundred feet of elevation in the Amazonas region east of the Andes. Along the Pacific coast, land is often at sea level, though broken by the fingers of the lower slopes of the Andes reaching to the sea.

There are three main environmental zones in the country: Andean highlands, tropical rain forest, and the Pacific coastal lowlands zone. Given this range of ecosystems, Ecuador is rated as the eighth most biodiverse country in the world, and indeed is one of seventeen "mega-diverse" countries on the planet. There is a good network of roads and a huge array of travel options, so you can quite easily reach most of the locations that interest you—but more of that in the "travelogue" of destinations below.

Ecuador contains almost 24,000 species of plants, 1618 species of birds, 366 species of mammals, 374 species of reptiles, and 460 species of amphibians (all frogs). However, habitat destruction from logging, mining, and oil extraction is seriously threatening the viability of much of this diversity. As you plan your visit, you can update yourself on the struggles over protecting the full range of diversity in Ecuador, including the Galapagos Islands.

Throughout Ecuador, the US dollar is the currency. There are automated teller machines everywhere, and they are compatible with major systems. However, notify your bank before you leave that you will be traveling internationally, so that they can release funds to you. Also, use passwords that are only four figures. Travelers' checks are no longer used.

As for language, if your Spanish can meet the challenge of counting to ten and then by hundreds; if you can use standard pleasantries for time of day, for the bill ("*la cuenta, por favor*"), and for "thank you" and "please"; and if you are prepared to live in the moment when things go a little more slowly than you expect, you will be fine. One of those small "South American Spanish" books can be useful, because there are a number of terms that differ from the high school Spanish that you took years ago. Also, in terms of your own manner in interacting with people if any difficulty arises, the firm, almost authoritarian approach that gets things done in North America or Europe is ineffective in Ecuador. People just smile and melt away. So you just smile and explain the problem, ask what they may suggest could be done, and the deeply ingrained politeness and kindness of Ecuadoreans will have an opportunity to be fully expressed.

WEATHER AND CLOTHING

For your trip to the mainland, your lightweight Galapagos clothes will meet most of your needs for the rain forest and coast, with some modifications as described below. But for Quito and the highlands, there are rather different requirements for being comfortable and safe. For the highlands, the weather tends to be around 20 degrees Celsius (in the high 60s Fahrenheit) in the day, but it gets much cooler at night. That's when the colorful jacket you buy on your first day at a market in Quito or in the major market town of Otavalo comes into its own. Also for your trips into the country, a lightweight waterproof jacket or windbreaker is essential, and in the rain forest a raincoat, or one of those inexpensive "capes," can come in handy.

Protection from the sun is a must—it is astounding how quickly you can burn at altitude, and don't forget to protect your hands. Naturally, one of those large, floppy iconic intrepid traveler hats, with a wide brim and a good chin strap, is an essential item to include.

Assuming you're going to the Galapagos as well, the travel tips for personal items in that section of chapter 5 apply here.

As for visits to the rain forest, unlike the Galapagos, this is not a place for tank tops and shorts. In the rain forest, you still will want to wear a big, lightweight hat, and here you will be glad for a long-sleeved lightweight, loose-fitting shirt; and long pants. Bring two or three of each, because they will get soaked and it is hard for them to dry. Do not take jeans; try to bring clothing that wicks moisture away from your skin. I tuck the pants into mid-length socks, so that no unwelcome crawling things can visit me. It's not stylish, but it works. I even put my shoes on my bed, protected by the mosquito netting, so that I won't get any surprises when I put them on in the morning. For shoes, the lodges will supply rubber boots for muddy forest walks, or you may wear running shoes if you don't mind them getting totally soggy. Mosquito repellent is a must for the rain forest and travel along the coast.

Even if you've packed sparsely and efficiently, taking into account overlap with Galapagos gear, you will have different sets of clothes—for sunny Galapagos, damp rain forest, and chilly highlands—and you certainly won't want to haul them everywhere you go. Your home

hotel back in Quito or Guayaquil will have a checked-bag service so you can take just what you need for a given segment of the trip, and there will be a safe box for any small valuables. It's likely that after your rain-forest jaunt you will want to have everything washed. There are laundries every few blocks in cities of any size, and the service is fast, dependable, and also likely to be much less expensive than what you will find in the hotel. So there is some packing and repacking after each travel segment, but at least you don't have to carry all the various sets of clothes to every destination.

Don't worry if you've forgotten something or you lose something or your batteries run down. Quito and Guayaquil have every kind of store for everything anyone could need.

LEFT: *Moist highlands of the Andes' eastern slopes* RIGHT: *La Balbanera Church near Riobamba*

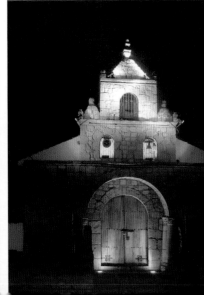

HEALTH PRECAUTIONS

There are no vaccinations required for entry into Ecuador. However, do consult your travel clinic about suggested prevention measures. While the rain forest is listed as a malaria area, wearing protective clothing as suggested (long-sleeved shirts, tucking pants in trousers, using bug repellent) is likely to reduce your risk of exposure. The places where you will be staying in the rain forest explicitly avoid having standing water or other mosquito breeding attractants around. The accommodations will have mosquito netting around the beds for nighttime protection. I do not advise either way on malaria medication. I have never used it myself, and find that few visitors I've known use it either. But it's a choice for you and your medical advisor.

Travel clinics near where I live in Vancouver, Canada, suggest the triple vaccine for typhoid, tetanus, and diphtheria. In the highlands in particular, you will be around farm animals where tetanus could be a risk if you get a cut or step on some sharp object. Consider getting the rabies vaccine also. There are lots of dogs wherever you go, many just running free, without apparent homes or regular care.

Whatever your choices, do bring your medical documentation for vaccines and for any health conditions you live with and the medications you take (i.e., for diabetes, drug allergies, insect bite reactions, etc.).

ARRIVAL AND ALTITUDE

When you are in Quito and the highlands, you may well suffer a bit from the effects of suddenly arriving at high altitudes. These effects include any one or more symptoms like headaches, tiring from the briefest walks, nausea, and difficulty sleeping. If you do have any of these discomforts, they'll likely go away within two or three days at the most. By walking slowly, eating moderately, drinking lots of fluids, and resting often, you should have little difficulty. If you smoke or drink alcohol, consider cutting back since cigarettes and alcohol both constrict oxygen to blood vessels.

You might want to consult with your doctor beforehand about any medications that can reduce headaches and aid with sleeping, but you can't know until you get there if you will even need these. At high altitudes I do usually have a dull headache, and I notice that I'm not scampering up stairs like I do back home, but for me and most of the folks I've traveled with, altitude is an inconvenience but not a problem. In Guayaquil there is the advantage of being at sea level, so altitude is not a consideration. You may have to adjust to the heat and humidity, but it's all part of the adventure.

17

TRAVELING THE ANDEAN HIGHLANDS

W hat strikes me most about traveling in the highlands is the bright clarity of the atmosphere at high altitudes and the constant change of stunningly beautiful scenery. Over the years and my many visits, the Andean highlands have become (for me) the equal of the Galapagos for their enchantment and sheer fascination. It has something to do with being anywhere from about 2400 to nearly 4300 meters (8000 to 14,000 feet) high, the air thin but clean, the sunshine so close, with every bend of the road showing another volcano, or a vast sweep of ranchland dotted with llamas, or a turquoise lake nestled in a volcanic crater. There is the possibility of seeing a condor, as I have, wheeling almost out of sight—but surely that is what it must have been.

In the highlands you'll see cowboys on wiry ponies, herding their flocks of sheep. There will be steep slopes checkered with tiny plots of land where the indigenous peoples grow potatoes or corn, scrabbling out a subsistence living. And you'll probably visit some of the huge haciendas, with their Spanish colonial mansions and rich land holdings in the valleys. (There have been some land reforms over the years, but the original owners continue to have the advantageous locations for farming, ranching, or now the very successful greenhouse-based production of roses for the international market.) You can see the most up-to-date farm machinery wending its way across fields. Then you look up the slope a ways and see tiny figures of men and women in traditional dress hacking with adzes into the soil of their own tiny pieces of land, or women and girls washing clothing on rocks by a stream.

HACIENDA-HOPPING

A highland trip should include "hacienda-hopping," spent in several different lodgings, as you travel from place to place over at least five or six days. A number of the haciendas have been converted into *hosterías* or more elaborate hotels, and they are beautiful, restful, often historic places. The buildings may be hundreds of years old, with family heirlooms and photo albums to leaf through to learn about the history of the hacienda and the surrounding area.

The classic haciendas are built on an open square plan, enclosing formal gardens, with a chapel along one side, equipment or tool rooms on another, and rooms for visitors along the front and other side. A large central living room offers a place to share in the evenings, with a fireplace, comfortable chairs, books, and a desk and computer. Wi-Fi is generally available. Breakfasts are always provided, and many of the larger accommodations have full-scale restaurants for lunches or dinners. It's also possible to drop in on a hacienda for meals as you continue on your travels in the highlands.

Most of the haciendas have nearby trails for easy walking on your own, and many offer horseback riding. The haciendas usually can arrange for guides for touring villages and markets around the area, for birding, or going to special historic or natural history sites.

Eco-Lodges in the Highlands

There are also "eco-lodges" in the highlands, which vary from luxurious accommodations to simple hostels geared to budget-conscious travelers and

Cowboy (shepherd) in the chilly highlands near Cotopaxi

backpackers, or for climbers acclimatizing for an attempt to summit Chimborazo or other peaks. Some of the eco-lodges are hacienda-style, and some have been created especially for visitors exploring the natural and human history of the highlands. They will have guides that can make sure you can follow up on your interests in hiking, birding, horseback riding, or local history and culture.

Many of the national parks or bio-reserves have eco-lodges. There are also a number of privately held reserves, which have their own visitor accommodations, array of activities, and guiding services for hikers, birders, photographers, or

Violet-ear hummingbird, spotted at a bed-and-breakfast

botanical enthusiasts. Again, because the country is so small, you can travel from place to place within a two- or three-hour drive at the most—having your own driver and guide or hiring a car and striking out on your own.

There are also more and more small, family-run bed-and-breakfast accommodations, which can be delightful places to stay, explore the local environment, eat local food, and just relax at your own pace. It can be wonderful to sit on the patio with your binoculars, camera, and a cup of local cinnamon tea (*canelazo*) while watching hummingbirds come to the feeders that your hosts have set out.

Market Towns in the Highlands

The highlands are the place to see markets and market towns. Some have a wide array of choices and some specialize in particular kinds of products. The internationally known Otavalo market specializes in clothing and weavings, or you can visit smaller village markets known for special items: Cotacachi for leather, Peguche for internationally known weavings, Cayambe for brick oven-baked sweet biscuits, Pelileo for jeans, or San Antonio de Ibarra for intricate carvings of religious figures. Some markets are open daily, but some are open only one day a week. You will want to plan for these visits, so that you don't come when a market isn't active. Latacunga is a large and very diverse market, open on Tuesdays and Saturdays. Other notable weekly markets include Pujuli (Wednesdays), Saquisili (Thursdays), and Guamote, a very traditional indigenous market (Thursdays).

Markets and other human-intensive sights and activities are wonderful, but the highlands also are rich with opportunities to observe and explore the natural world. There are national parks and biosphere reserves, the birding is excellent, and much of the plant life is unique, both in terms of species diversity and in the miniaturization that occurs at these altitudes.

Looking Forward to the Highlands

Assuming that your travel is by car, with a driver and guide to make the best use of your time, a typical five- or six-day ramble in the highlands would give you the opportunity to experience the highlights of the communities and countryside described below. You may not get to all of them, and indeed there are many comparable alternatives in the highlands environment, but the descriptions below will give you an idea of what you can look forward to. It also may serve as a foundation for planning a variation in your travels, discussing options with other travelers you may be going with, or with your travel company, or your guide once you are in Ecuador.

Though more and more travelers to the Galapagos come and go out of Guayaquil, it is easy to fly to Quito either before or after your island sojourn. Guayaquil is likely to be your entry and exit point from Ecuador (even if you are going to the Galapagos). From Quito it's an easy transition to a trip through the highlands surrounding the city and then traveling south to Guayaquil and the coastal region.

18

QUITO AND ENVIRONS

. . . .

You will want to spend as much time as possible in Quito, given its beauty and historic significance as a World Cultural Heritage Site. Quito is so large, so varied in its character, with so many sights, sounds, and places to visit, that it really is best to have a guide with you. Yet you also should plan for some free time, to return to places that particularly pleased you, to sit at an outdoor cafe, or do some people-watching or birding in one of the parks.

Quito is a safe city generally, but as in any travel situation around the world, especially in crowded conditions with lots of well-off tourists, you should take reasonable precautions. These include carrying most of your money in a concealed pouch that you can have ready access to, not carrying free-hanging purses or cameras attached only by a little cord to your wrist, and not leaving your cell phone on the table when you go to the facilities. And avoid traveling alone at night in places that have few other people around.

It is quite easy to get around on your own in Quito—taxis are plentiful and inexpensive, walking is generally safe, and many of your destinations will be within a short taxi ride or walking distance from each other. There is a tramcar system also. But for the best use of your time overall, I suggest that you arrange for a guide for much of each day. There are many thoroughly trained, licensed guides, and your tour company will have connected you to one of them from the time you get off the plane. (If you are traveling independently, your hotel or the offices of Quito-based touring companies can be a good source of guides; just make sure they are licensed ones.) In my experience guides are unfailingly well informed, personable, and helpful, especially during emergencies such as illnesses or lost luggage or missed flights. They will be pleased to advise you about how best to spend your free time—

cafes, parks to visit, shopping–they know it all, are intensely proud of their country and their city. Guides will do all they can to make your visit even better than you imagined it could be. In my ten visits to Quito over the years, I have always found this to be true.

Quito is a long, narrow city, located at 2800 meters (about 9200 feet), in a river valley squeezed in between mountains taller than 5200 meters (17,000 feet). The city stretches along the eastern side of the Pichincha volcano. Quito is known as the City of Four Seasons; its weather can change quite rapidly. Because of its high elevation, the temperatures are generally cool in the daytime, but can approach freezing levels at night. I always carry a lightweight hooded jacket with me, usually buying a perfect one at one of the local markets within hours of my arrival. Remember, you are much nearer the sun here, and the valley is very dry, so sunscreen and skin and lip creams are a very good idea. And don't forget to drink lots of water–high-altitude sickness may affect you, and keeping hydrated is the easiest way to avoid it from the start.

Quito is a comfortable and quite safe city to walk in, assuming you use the standard precautions for being just about anywhere these days–don't flash money around, don't leave electronic equipment on the table while you head to the bar, eschew dangly purses or large wallets stuffed into a back pocket. At night, stay in well-lit areas with a

Quito bike-lending station

reasonable number of locals and tourists who are themselves out taking walks, shopping, eating, going to clubs or theatres. It is a good idea to take taxis at night, to avoid getting a bit lost and just as an added security in a big city that you won't know very well.

The World Cultural Heritage that is Quito is all around you, so how best to experience that heritage, to learn about it, to enjoy it? As with all of the Spanish colonial cities, it is centered around several large plazas, each with its own monumental, historic buildings, with the cathedrals being the most dramatic. There are some forty churches, sixteen monasteries and convents, and seventeen plazas, many within walking distance or a short taxi ride from each other. Start your visit with the Old Town, colonial Quito.

THE PLAZA GRANDE

The Plaza de la Independencia (Plaza Grande) is the anchor point of most visits to Quito. On the other three sides of the Plaza Grande are the Governor's Palace, the Archbishop's Palace, and the City Hall, and what is now the Metropolitan Cultural Center, in the angle between the cathedral and the Governor's Palace.

The Archbishop's Palace has an airy courtyard, with a very attractive open-air cafe and some "artisanal" gift shops, with traditional arts and crafts.

The Metropolitan Cultural Center was the first University in Quito, established by the Jesuits, and now is a museum of colonial art. There is a small admission fee to the museum and it also has contemporary art exhibitions. The museum itself is open Tuesdays through Sundays, for a very small admission fee, which is even less for students or seniors. The municipal library is integrated into the building. The building has a courtyard with a pyramid-style large skylight with a very bright and welcoming cafe.

LA COMPAÑÍA DE JESUS (THE CATHEDRAL OF QUITO)

Quito's cathedral, La Compañía de Jesus, is just one block away from the Plaza Grande. The cathedral was first constructed between 1562 and 1565, but has been damaged, rebuilt, and expanded over the centuries in response to earthquakes, volcanoes, and changing church policies and practices. This great building is the jewel of Quito and the best sample of Baroque style in Latin America. The cathedral is staggeringly ornate, with some two tons of gold leaf covering seemingly every surface. Its design has evolved over time, and is a mixture of neoclassical, Mudéjar, Baroque, and Gothic art.

The cathedral is open all day Monday through Saturday, but only on afternoons on Sundays. There is a small entrance fee, which includes guide services within the building itself; by adding a little more you can go up to the cupolas. Your own guide will have a lot to tell you about the history, structure, and current usage of this edifice.

SAN FRANCISCO CHURCH

There is an even larger plaza, the Plaza of the San Francisco church, just two blocks from the Plaza Grande. The San Francisco church and its monastery comprise the oldest buildings in Quito. The church was founded by the Franciscan order, with construction beginning in 1535 and ending some hundred years later (dates tend to be imprecise). It is the largest religious complex in South America, covering more than 3 hectares (two full city blocks). There is a fan-shaped staircase leading into the church, apparently designed to cause those entering to lower their heads to be careful of their steps, and ensuring they entered the church with their heads bowed. The courtyard of the main cloister has a formal garden, with wide winding pathways and complex beds of greenery. The church is an active place of worship, and is open to the public in between services all day long from Monday to Saturday, and in the afternoons on Sunday.

The Plaza is also the home of a Museum of Colonial Art, the oldest museum in Quito, and in the San Francisco church complex itself there is a museum of artwork in the collection of the Franciscan order.

CASA DEL ALABADO MUSEUM (MUSEUM OF PRAISE)

Also well worth visiting in the Old Town is the Casa del Alabado Museum, which takes you back to pre-Incan times. Located half a block from Plaza San Francisco, between that plaza and Santa Clara Plaza, the museum is housed in a building dating from the late seventeenth century, but within those traditional walls is a truly impressive, innovative, and attractive approach to preservation and education. Completed in 2011, this museum was one of the highlights of my latest visit to Quito. The museum is named for an inscription on the façade of the house that says, "Praised be the holy soul, the façade of this house was finished in the year of the lord 1671."

The museum has a collection of some five thousand precolonial, pre-Inca artifacts, with only one-tenth of these on display. Some are as old as five thousand years! The emphasis is on interpreting the

Plaza Grande, Independence Square, Quito

cultural lives of the people, of how they saw themselves, how they portrayed themselves in both naturalistic and symbolic forms. In precontact times, the peoples of the area conceptualized their universe in three worlds: the Upper, Middle, and Lower. Their art reflects this belief, and the museum is organized according to these principles. The pieces range from animals, to humans at work and play, to sexually proud beings, to containers for symbolic or practical use (pitchers, cups, bowls).

The displays are very well signed, and because the museum actively encourages archaeological work and study throughout

Ecuador, there is an exhibit of how this kind of work is done. I particularly liked the display of a dig, where set in the floor, covered with heavy glass, is a reproduction of the kind of archaeological excavation that uncovered many of the artifacts. You can see the different strata of earth, the tools at the bottom, a few artifacts themselves. It brings the whole process to life. While all of these museums have websites that readers will no doubt review, I particularly recommend that of this museum, because of how it explains and displays the collection.

CASA MUSEO MARIA AUGUSTA URRUTIA

Just a few steps from the Plaza Grande, the Casa Museo Maria Augusta Urrutia places you in the midst of early-twentieth-century Quito. It was the home of the Urrutia family for nearly one hundred years, until the death of Señora Urrutia in 1987. The family were very wealthy, of the aristocracy of Quito society. Throughout her life, Señora Urrutia devoted her energies and her wealth to assisting the poor, in particular, helping homeless children. She left a foundation as a legacy to continue her efforts.

Her home has been preserved as an example of upper-class life especially in the early 1900s. This was an era when a house such as this had the very latest in plumbing and electricity, along with wood-burning stoves, a cold storage room, and even a milling machine for making their own flour. Decorated with a wealth of stained glass windows, hand-painted wallpaper, and fascinating wall murals, the home is largely furnished with ornate European pieces. There are family articles and mementos artfully displayed, almost as if the family were just in another room and will be coming to welcome you at any moment. There also is an excellent collection of Ecuadorean art from Señora Urrutia's times, especially by her favorite artist, Victor Midero.

The front of the house is aligned with the continuous facings of other buildings in the street, in the colonial style. And in the same style, as you enter the museum there is a large courtyard, with the home built around it and beyond it. There is a small entry fee and English-speaking guides (or your own). There is also interpretive signage in English. This is a peaceful, fascinating place to be, to see how the upper crust lived, in a style now past.

GUAYASAMÍN MUSEUM AND LA CAPILLA DEL HOMBRE (THE CHAPEL OF MAN)

Oswaldo Guayasamín (1919–1999) was Ecuador's most famous modern painter. He came from a very poverty-stricken family, and while his artistic talents brought him wealth and fame, he concentrated his work on portraying the suffering of the disenfranchised. He willed his own extensive private art collection to the city of Quito, and it is on display in the residence part of his home. He used his name and resources to form a foundation that promotes a wide variety of cultural activities—concerts, workshops, events. The museum is a part of what was his private residence. It has beautiful gardens as well as his own collection of pre-Columbian, colonial, and contemporary art. There is a small entry fee, and a guide will be provided for you.

Virtually next door to the museum is La Capilla del Hombre (The Chapel of Man). It is architecturally very distinctive, built as a kind of abstraction of an Incan temple. There are two levels, each having murals and massive paintings by Guayasamín, as well as posted quotations from him about oppression and inequality, especially that of children. Many of the works are reminiscent, but not derivative, of Picasso's *Guernica*. The building itself, and the powerful works of art within it, have a great emotional impact, and the feelings and the message will stay with you for a long time.

La Capilla is open Tuesday through Sunday. Admission is free on Sundays, with a minimal charge other days. The chapel is about a 25-minute taxi ride from central Quito. It is a good idea to ask your driver to wait for you, for an hour or so. They are willing to do this and do not charge very much. Agree on a rate before you start out, and tips will always be welcome. I found that this worked very well.

THE WATER MUSEUM (YAKU PARQUE, MUSEO DEL AGUA)

The Water Museum, opened in 2005, is designed to inform visitors about water, the mainstay of life. *Yaku* is the Quechua word for water. The museum traces the sources of water to the Quito area, and tells about the history of water storage, treatment, conservation, and current usage.

Archaeological reproduction at Casa del Alabado Museum, Quito

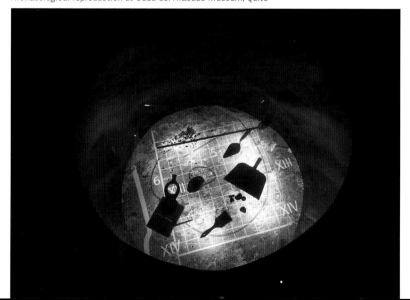

The remains of Quito's first water reservoir, where water distribution began in 1913, are surrounded by beautiful gardens. Several permanent displays tell about the chemical makeup of water, its importance to the natural world, and its relationship to humans. There is also a section on water in our homes, about our responsibility for sustaining this key to our existence.

Located at the base of Pichincha, in the El Placer neighborhood, the museum offers a 180-degree view of the city stretching out below, with the beginning of the natural world of the mountainside behind you. If you are traveling with children, they will especially enjoy the museum's interactive displays. The museum is open Tuesdays through Sundays, from 9:00 AM to 5:00 PM. There is a modest fee, reduced for young children and seniors. Take a taxi there, for a 20-minute ride.

THE MIDDLE OF EARTH (MITAD DEL MUNDO)—INTIÑAN AND THE OBELISK

Ecuador is, after all, a national namesake of the equator, and Quito celebrates this in many ways, including two rather diverse museums. One is privately owned, and the other is operated by the city of Quito. Both are open to the public for a modest fee. You can reach them by taxi or bus, or through your own tour services; they are about a 45-minute drive from downtown Quito.

Intiñan (Path of the Sun) has over the years developed into a rather interesting collection of displays of pre-Incan and current indigenous life, with small three-dimensional representations portraying peoples in their everyday settings. The museum has a little guinea pig enclosure, and a replica of an archaeological dig, with assorted artifacts.

Intiñan is the location of the true equator, and you will not want to miss the chance to have your picture taken straddling both hemispheres. If you are a plant person, you will love the surroundings here, the high desert all around you with various beautiful cacti; some were in bloom when I was there in March. Some are spiky, some curving, often having a kind of downy covering, which helps conserve water.

The birdlife is not rich, but you will have really good, close views of the rufous-collared sparrow, a handsome bird with a perky song. I think of it as the "totemic" bird of Quito and the highlands, seeming to be there at every turn.

The other museum (known locally as the Obelisk), just a few minutes' drive from Intiñan, is focused on a very large equator monument, a trapezoidal, 30-meter-high (98 feet) plinth with the inevitable globe on the top. There are stairs up to the top and full views of the Quito valley. There is an ethnographic museum, under a big colorful dome. There is an additional small fee to enter.

The whole complex has wide pathways, and a plaza surrounded by numerous gift shops, containing a mix of qualities and types of traditional and contemporary craft styles. There are also guides who tell you about the differences in energies and

Seniors' fitness area, Parque El Ejido, Quito

impacts of gravity in the two hemispheres. They demonstrate how water flows in a different direction down a drain, depending on which side of the equator you are standing. The explanation is a bit nebulous and the water does get a subtle nudge, but it's fun. Of course, there is a line drawn on the ground along what is supposed to be the equator, though in reality it is some 240 meters (800 feet) from there.

Both museums are open every day of the week.

EL EJIDO AND PARQUE CAROLINA— BOTANICAL GARDEN AND VIVARIUM

When I am in Quito, I always make sure to go to two of the many parks—the very large Parque Carolina and the smaller El Ejido ("commons land"). El Ejido is at the southern end of Amazonas Avenue and is a few minutes' walk from the many shops and hotels of the main part of the New Town, where you are very likely to be staying. The park is very much a family park, very quiet in spite of the traffic surrounding it, with lots of playgrounds for kids and benches to sit on and enjoy some time for yourself.

When I was last there, the friend I was with, a born Quiteña, pointed out the seniors' fitness section. It happens that a recent vice-president of the country became paraplegic, after receiving a gunshot wound, and this sensitized him to the challenges facing persons with disabilities. He created a number of changes in legislation and policies to have a more equitable treatment of persons with disabilities. One of his contributions was the establishment of a special seniors' fitness area in every large park.

These areas have a complete set of every kind of fitness equipment that you would find in any fancy gym or club, only the equipment is modified so that it does not require electrical power and is so sturdy it can withstand all kinds of weather—and it's free. We sat and watched seniors on treadmills (using rollers, like the luggage

chutes in airport), seniors working on their upper-body strength with their own bodies providing the resistance, seniors using big wheels to extend arm and shoulder flexibility, or standing on twisting disks to limber up their back and lower body. All these exercises were being done on brilliantly colored machines. A large sign at the edge of the area explains the purpose of each piece and how to use it. This seems to me a great example of a city supporting healthy aging, especially for people with limited incomes.

At the other end of Amazonas is Parque Carolina. To get there I took about a 30-minute walk from the center of the New Town, checking out the many shops, malls, and bookstores along the way. One of the most interesting things about the walk was having a chance to talk with the people in charge of the kiosk for the bike-loan program in Quito. I'd seen people using sturdy white bicycles, with the Q symbol of Quito on the back wheel guard. People can check bikes in and out at the attractive kiosks (which provide jobs for people), scattered through town. There are excellent booklets explaining the system, advising on safe biking practices, describing the various street signs. I was impressed: another example of a city supporting healthy living and environmental sustainability. Not that I'd ever have the nerve to bicycle in

Carnivorous pitcher plant, Botanical Garden, Parque Carolina, Quito

Quito traffic—it's too fast, and the streets are far too circuitous for me!

The Parque itself is 67 hectares (65.5 acres), similar to New York City's Central Park in its size, location in the midst of a major urban center, and diverse usage. Many events are held there, and artists display their works. There's a pond where you can rent paddle boats, a skateboard area, courts for playing "ecua-volley," room for kids to run and play, or benches for all to sit down and just enjoy life. Birders will find it of interest, and can find a guidebook to the birds of Quito in the larger bookstores, such as Libri Mundi.

Parque Carolina is also home to two very special ecological centers, the Botanical Garden and the Vivarium, both on the western side of the park. The Botanical Garden has two large orchid houses, where you can wander at your leisure, learn their names and typical habitat, and take pictures. The Botanical Garden also houses examples of various ecosystems, like a beautiful *paramo* room, complete with a pond and a very lively Andean coot! (I don't know how it got there, and it may have passed on into the Andean heavens by the time you visit, but the plant life is still fascinating.) There is also a collection of carnivorous plants, just waiting for an unsuspecting insect to fall into their waiting suspended cups or being caught by their sticky little hairs.

The Vivarium, just a few steps from the garden buildings, is a most unusual rescue, breeding, research, and exhibition facility, dedicated to the amphibians and reptiles of Ecuador. This diverse country has some 460 species of frogs and 210 species of snakes. In this small building are a number of glass-fronted mini-environments, homes for different species of frog. The rooms are kept quite dark, so that the nonhuman inhabitants won't be disturbed by being observed (no picture-taking allowed). Some of the frogs are easy to see through the long windows, clinging to vines, or partially submerged in their little ponds. But for some you have to look very carefully, because once ensconced in foliage, their camouflage makes them just disappear.

The Vivarium has an active educational program, and when there I was surrounded by excited children as I listened to the guide explain about the denizens of the various environments. An active research and resources facility, the Vivarium has some eight thousand titles in its library. It also provides an important health service, in that some of the poisonous snakes are "milked" of their venom, which is then developed into anti-snakebite treatments. This is a very important source in Ecuador for this vital substance; otherwise the anti-venom serum has to be imported at a very high cost.

There is a small gift shop, with proceeds going toward the upkeep of the Vivarium. It has to be self-supporting, because it is not funded by the government. The shop offers very appealing gifts, all with an amphibian theme, as well as both scientific and story books on the amphibian world.

HANGING OUT IN QUITO

Two of the most interesting areas for just rambling around Quito on your own, or with a small unguided group, are the Marischal district and La Ronda Street. La Marischal, in the New Town area near Avenue Foch, is Quito's entertainment hub, open late into the night, where there are open-air cafes, great shopping, and the ever-popular seeing and being seen—for locals as well as tourists.

La Ronda Street is the place for strolling and absorbing the Quito ambience. It is a cobbled street just off the Plaza Santo Domingo in the Old Town. La Ronda has been carefully rejuvenated to recreate authentic colonial facades to the buildings, yet each building has a distinctive interior for its cafes or shops. The interiors are of a "modern" cast, but they must stay within the guidelines for internal changes that are allowed by Quito and World Heritage Site standards. La Ronda was rebuilt with national and international support, which encouraged local participation in its development and the benefits from that.

And for just plain fun, take the Teleférico, the cable car with roomy gondolas that goes up the side of Pichincha volcano. It is one of the highest aerial rides in the world, and you will go from 3117 meters (10,226 feet) to 4112 meters (13,490 feet). If measured horizontally, from the base to the top, the distance is 2237 linear meters (7339 feet). It is a scary ride, but delightful. At the landing you'll find a cafe and also restrooms. There is a well-marked gravel trail where you can have a view of the entire sweep of Quito below you. The view really dramatizes the challenges that people have faced for millennia to build a community that has to be sandwiched between massive volcanoes.

If you want to go even higher, you can follow an extension of the trail to the summit of Pichincha. It is also possible to rent a horse for a guided trip to the top. The walk can take up to three hours or so each way; the horseback ride takes about half that time. Be sure you have layers of warm clothing, a windbreaker, and a nice warm hat with ear flaps (so easy to buy in any market). You can take a short taxi ride to the foot of the Teleférico from most places you are likely to be in Quito, and there are usually taxis below for your ride back—ask the driver the price, and check out more than one if you feel you should.

19

HIGHLANDS NORTH OF QUITO

ravel in the highlands or any-where in Ecuador is more than moving from one visitor destination to another, because everywhere you go you will have spontaneous encounters or sights that happen but once and are remembered forever.

During my latest visit, as we were driving out of Quito toward Otavalo, we happened to stop at a large gas station complex, for gas, snacks, and a restroom. The station was located near a small stream, with pathways leading to a school, and some small houses. A young woman along the path was doing some beautiful embroidery on a small wooden hoop. She was in traditional Otavaleño dress, with a long skirt, embroidered white blouse, black scarf used as a headdress, and strings of golden necklaces. She chatted with our guide and suddenly broke into song, singing two lively but brief songs in Quechua, the language of the majority of indigenous people. Our guide explained

that these were traditional folk songs. The young woman had a lovely voice. She also explained, via our guide, that the way a shawl is worn indicates whether or not a woman is married. When it is worn only on one side, the left one, that means that a woman is not married. We also were shown how the black scarf worn by all adult women can be turned into the traditional head covering for women. So there was a "cultural moment" just as we paused along the road.

Quito is also a base for some very interesting day trips for birding or spending some quiet time in one of the small traditional villages nearby. Talk with your travel agent, or with the staff where you are staying, to decide on at least one or two day trips to extend your enjoyment in Ecuador.

NATURE NEAR QUITO—MINDO CLOUD FOREST RESERVE

Only a couple of hours drive northwest of Quito is the Tandayapa Valley, which

Blue-gray tanager in the Mindo Cloud Forest

includes several small communities within the cloud forest ecosystem on the western slopes of the Andes. The cloud forests are created because as the moist winds from the Pacific Ocean rise up the western Andean slopes, the air cools and it precipitates in the form of extensive clouds and frequent rains. The altitude of cloud forests ranges from about 1100 meters (3600 feet) up to about 5000 meters (16,400 feet). The valley is heaven for bird-watchers, where there are a number of eco-lodges around the community of Mindo.

Just 17 miles north of Quito, on the way to Mindo, you should stop for a while at the Pululahua Geobotanical Reserve.

There are trails, mountain biking, and marvelous views of the farmland, forests and valleys of the Pululahua volcano that gives the reserve its name. From the main road you also can visit the very interesting Butterfly Farm. There you can see the full cycle of reproduction of butterflies, with plenty of chances to photograph them.

The community of Mindo is within the Mindo–Nambillo Cloud Forest reserve, a nationally protected area of 19,200 hectares (47,400 acres). The town itself is at 1250 meters (4100 feet) altitude, so you probably won't feel fatigued as you walk along the many trails, or stop to view birds while at a cafe or viewpoint by the road. If your time is limited, you will want to have a birding expert to guide you, and to have a car and driver (so your guide is free to spot birds as you're driven along the winding roads). I was with a very good birder who also had a deep knowledge of the overall natural history and geology of the whole area, so I felt I had made the most of the day. You can arrange for a similar adventure through your own guide or hotel, or in tourism companies in Quito. Of course, if you have time to stay in one of the many eco-lodges they will have local birding experts.

I had some of the most exciting birding moments of my latest visit to the mainland on a day trip to Mindo, where there were bird feeders everywhere in one of the eco-lodges we visited briefly. There were sliced, ripe bananas fixed to the branches of nearby trees and humming-bird feeders suspended from the eaves of the rustic building. In just half an hour, in that one small area, barely moving from our vantage points, I saw thirty-four different species, including a toucan bar-bet, six species of tanagers, and fifteen kinds of hummingbirds. It was also some-how touching to see warblers I know from birding every year in eastern Canada, warblers that make the long migration from South America to Canada, to breed in the northern summer. I looked down the slope a bit, and there was the Canada warbler, with its yellow throat and stringy black bib. There were blue-gray tanagers, and a longer stay would have revealed many other migrants as well.

The Mindo area is a major recre-ational center, concentrated on the fast-flowing Rio Blanco. You'll find zip lines, river rafting, tubing, rappeling, canyoning, mountain biking, and many levels of hiking. There are tour compa-nies that can arrange these adventures, or you can make arrangements on your own with eco-lodges or tour companies in Mindo.

Another excellent area for birding is around Bella Vista, where there is a private reserve and simple overnight accommodations for visitors in the cloud forest lodge there. You can arrange with your hotel or tour company for an expert birder guide, driver, and car.

CAYAMBE

A brief, but very enjoyable place to visit along the drive north of Quito is Cayambe. Here several bakeries make flaky, slightly curled sweet biscuits that go very well with coffee or hot chocolate. In the open area of the shop, just the other side of the service counter, you can watch bakers rolling out the dough and cutting it into biscuits. These are then put on baking tins set on a long-handled plank and inserted into a ceiling-high, open-faced brick oven. They bake for only a few moments in the intense heat, and come out as delicious *biscochos*. It reminded me of bakeries in Old Montreal, where the genuine water bagels are hand-made, put on long boards, and slipped into open ovens.

OTAVALO

Otavalo is surely the most famous of all the market towns, and it can easily take half a day to see it all, including having lunch at one of the many cafes in the area. Look for signs saying "traditional Ecuadorean food," which will tend to be grilled chicken, fresh veggies, and an excellent salad. Grilled guinea pig may be on the menu, though visitors differ in how appealing this may be.

Otavalo is the place to shop for locally made garments—sweaters, jackets, pants, gloves, handbags, shawls, scarves, jewelry. These are "artisanal" products, ones that draw on traditional methods and motifs, though they also evolve in response to the tastes and interests of their clientele—

international travelers. For example, over the last thirty-five years I've seen sweaters and jackets change from basic knits, simple styles, and a narrow range of colors, to quite stylish shapes and dramatic colors, using a variety of complex woven patterns. Purses used to be simply string bags, and now they are almost "designer" style, using combinations of woven material and leathers, with compartments for laptops, iPhones, and GPS units.

You are expected to bargain in the Otavalo market and wherever there are goods that visitors are likely to buy and take home—like clothing, carvings, paintings, even toys. It's not a tough bargaining process, with either side trying to take the most advantage of the other, but more of

Tapestries and weavings at the Otavalo market

a friendly exchange. Generally you ask how much something is, and indeed if you find that price reasonable, you can buy it right away. But the customary next step is for you to suggest perhaps 25 percent less. The vendor will go up to half of the remaining difference—so it starts at $20, you've said $15, the vendor says $17, and you probably accept that. You also have the option of saying thanks, but no thanks, and wandering away. Usually the vendor will call after you and lower their original price and you go through the process again.

There is one thing that may make you uneasy at first, but which is not a problem at all. That is, vendors in markets such as Otavalo don't keep a lot of change right at hand, and it is common for them to have to get change from another vendor's stall a few rows away. They will tell you this and dash away. It may take a few minutes, and you may start to worry. But they *will* be back! They are honest and also can hardly desert their stall just to walk off with your $20 bill. (All transactions are in US dollars and the bills must be fairly new, not written on or torn, so that vendors—and you—can be sure they are genuine.)

There is even more to Otavalo than shopping for yourself and for presents for folks back home. This highland community has a very large food market as well. Everything is very meticulously set out—pyramids of cherries, banks of bananas, open sacks of different kinds of

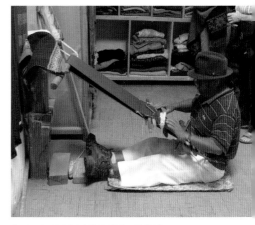

A weaver at a backstrap loom at José Cotacachi's workshop in Peguche

beans, peas, potatoes, huge carrots piled like colorful logs. The meat section is not for the vegetarian or otherwise faint of heart—pigs' heads with grinning teeth and staring eyes; trays of entrails on the way to the garbage or becoming sausages; bright yellow chicken carcasses, feet and heads attached. Not at all like the disembodied meat sections so common in mega-grocery stores in the home countries of visitors.

It seems that the fruit and vegetable vendors tend to be women, and the meat handlers and vendors are men. The markets are also family affairs, with even very young children standing guard on the racks of clothing, or rearranging the fruit, or helping to sort out the beans to make sure that no stones or other debris are present. The younger ones also may have a toy with them, and they can wander here and there when not engaged in the family business.

While the Sunday market is the biggest and most colorful, it's open daily on a much smaller and more intimate scale. Often it's just as good to come here on the weekdays. Bargaining with visitors is not a big feature here, though you can always ask the price and offer something a bit lower. If you are price-conscious, you may find that on the off-days the prices are somewhat lower, to encourage buying when the market is less busy.

PEGUCHE

Just a short drive farther north is Peguche, the small tapestry town. I always visit the main weaving workshop there, run by internationally known weaver, José Cotacachi, and his fellow artisans. He sits on the bench of his loom, working away as the shuttle flies and the colors and designs evolve, while he chats with visitors. Sometimes he pauses to move to a small back-strap loom, showing how he works sitting on the floor, with the yarn looped around his back, with both yarn ends attached at the wall. The width of these back-strap loom tapestries is just 38 centimeters (15 inches) or so, but the pieces made from full-frame looms can be 1.2 meters (4 feet) wide and as long as needed for the design. José creates very abstract pieces or somewhat schematized plant and animal life portrayals, or ones reflecting ancient symbols, such as a twelve-square piece that contains the Incan calendar. It has been fascinating to see how the patterns have evolved over the years, and to see the continuation of a long-standing artisanal tradition. There is some bargaining here, as in Otavalo, but again, it is low-key and the tapestries will be well worth what you end up paying.

Just at the edge of town there is a waterfall that is sacred to the indigenous peoples. The waterfall is believed to be occupied by an evil spirit, and once a year, at Inti Raymi (St. Thomas, in the Catholic calendar), there are ceremonies and celebrations for driving the spirit away and keeping it away for the year to come. This is in June, and visitors do sometimes attend, usually with a guide.

The guides are bound to be familiar with the studio of a musician in Peguche who creates his own instruments—the small guitars made from armadillo skin, larger ones, and many kinds of flutes and panpipes. Visitors sit around on stools while he plays for them, explains how the various instruments work, and quickly makes an eight-tube panpipe. The hollow reed is cut to the different lengths, bound together with a kind of grass, the ends smoothed, and a beautiful tune comes pouring out. Sometimes the children of the family join in with singing and playing with their own instruments.

COTACACHI

Not far from Peguche is Cotacachi, the leather town, which specializes in the design and sales of all kinds of shoes and bags. Cotacachi has the only high school in the country that trains students in the full range of working with leather, whether for garments, riding equipment, purses or wallets. There are shops along the main street and a wonderful public art portrayal of a leather workshop, with statues of nearly life-sized workers, cutting and sewing leather goods.

It is a treat to spend the night in one of the haciendas in the area. We stayed in a large, Spanish colonial–style hacienda, built 150 years ago. There was a central building and a number of separate cottages. We walked around the grounds, enjoyed the extensive kitchen garden, peered at several llamas in a small corral, and chatted with other guests—all this within a two-hour drive from Quito.

20

HIGHLANDS SOUTH AND EAST OF QUITO

The Pan-American Highway follows what is called the Avenue of the Volcanoes. The eastern side of the Avenue includes Antisana, Llanganates, and Sangay national parks, each with volcanoes taller than 4570 meters (15,000 feet). To the west is the most well-known of the parks, Cotopaxi, named for its 5897-meter (19,347-foot) volcano. To the south is Cajas National Park.

Each of the national parks allows visitors to roam on their own, but for explorations of any depth, a guide is essential and access can be difficult without an all-wheel-drive vehicle to handle the rough mountain roads. Some of the parks have developed interpretive programs, including interpretive centers. There is a corps of naturalist guides who accompany visitors and who also monitor the safety of both people and the spectacular Andean *paramo*, with its fragile moist plains, hundreds of lakes, and forested volcanic slopes. This is a very positive change over

the last decade, as is a program of working with the indigenous people who live in the vast park areas, incorporating them into the protection of the environment and including them in economic activities, such as eco-tourism.

Check the website of each park and related sites to learn how accessible each is. Parks such as Llanganates can be explored almost exclusively via very carefully planned and well-led outdoor adventure guiding services. There are eco-lodges in some of the parks, and likely accommodations in nearby communities. Some will have their own guiding services or can connect you to others.

In my travels to the highlands I have always visited Cotopaxi National Park, and on my latest trip I spent a brief time in one area of Cajas. The descriptions below give just a hint of the marvelous experiences that you can have in any of Ecuador's national parks. The parks and reserves are true *tesoros*—treasures of planet Earth.

COTOPAXI NATIONAL PARK

I think it was on my first visit to Cotopaxi National Park that I fell in love with the highlands. Cotopaxi is 5897 meters (19,347 feet) high, the iconic volcanic mountain of Ecuador. Cotopaxi's glaciers are the primary source of fresh water for the surrounding area and for Quito. However, its glacial cap is noticeably shrinking, due to climate change. Aside from scientific measurement of these changes, I have my own informal records of this. There are snapshots of me and fellow travelers from my ten visits from 1981 through 2014. We stand smiling and windblown with the steadily diminishing Cotopaxi's glacier forming the backdrop of these happy moments.

Cotopaxi Park is just 50 kilometers (31 miles) south of Quito, and is easily reached by car. Non-Ecuadoreans need a special permission (*patente*) to enter the park. This can be done through one of the park guides at the entry, or a travel agency in Quito. This permit and the services of a trained local guide are part of the protection and conservation efforts for this marvelous environment.

The park is very well signed, with welcoming carved wooden maps of the park and explanations in both Spanish and English. At the park entrance, at about 3660 meters (12,000 feet) in altitude, you'll find an excellent gift shop—a great place to get sew-on patches or pins for your travel duds, or to buy an extra fleece jacket

The slopes of Cotopaxi, with receding glaciers

or cap, complete with the park's symbols stitched in. It's cold and often fairly windy and misty at these altitudes, so if you need some more layering, or just want something wonderful to take home, this is the place. The shop has restrooms also.

From here it's a 10-kilometer (6-mile) drive up to the combined interpretive center and museum, which has a wonderful three-dimensional table map of Cotopaxi. There are also posters, and hands-on displays explaining volcanic processes, including ones about nearby active volcanoes, such as the continuously puffing Tungurahua.

Along with our own tour guide, we were joined by one of the park's own naturalist guides. She was well-informed about the park's history, flora, fauna, and geology. It was good to be walking along with one of these guides, and to know we were actively supporting the ongoing efforts to conserve the environment through participation of the local peoples.

At the interpretive center area you'll find also a loop path through a botanical garden. This is an excellent opportunity to get a close look at the characteristic plants of the *paramo*—the high, moist plains of the Andean slopes. There is a smooth gravel trail, easily covered in a casual half hour. The labeling is clear and bilingual. It is fascinating to see the miniaturization of plants there, as they struggle against winds, cold, and thin soil. For example, in western Canada the columbine flower has stems as tall as 76

centimeters (30 inches) and flowers as wide as 5 centimeters (2 inches) across. In the paramo, the same flower is there, only about 7.5 centimeters (3 inches) tall and with the flower about 1 centimeter (0.5 inch) across. The same is true for what is known as the Indian paintbrush, a leggy plant of 45 centimeters (18 inches) or more in Canada, and about 10 centimeters (4 inches) tall in the paramo. There are blueberries of some sort, also hugging the ground, not standing bushes, and the berries are a quarter the size of the wild ones in Canada.

Limpiopungo's Paramo

Another beautiful place to spend some time in Cotopaxi is at Limpiopungo, a small lake at 3830 meters (12,565 feet) in elevation. There is a path around it, and the paramo stretches out on all sides, with mountain ridges rising from there. The walk is fairly level, with just a slight rise now and then, and it takes about an hour and a half of walking, stopping, taking pictures, seeing birds, walking again. Of course, at this altitude you are unlikely to be able to set a brisk pace, much less stick to one. But why would you? The views are stunning, there is an open-air but covered viewpoint along the way, and the birding is riveting.

The paramo is the home of the Andean lapwing, a relative of plovers of North America or the lapwing of England. It is as large as a small gull, a pale gray that makes it hard to pick out in the grassy expanses of paramo, but when it moves, you will notice it. In the lake were several Andean teals, dabbling away. There were also Andean versions of coots, of pintail ducks, of gulls. In the grass was a tiny plumbeous sierra finch, also a dull gray-blue, spotted only as it flew from here to there and finally landed to feed. A solitary sandpiper flew over; a cinclode with its striped eye and dusky brown body sang a lovely song as it picked and pecked along the ground; and overhead a bar-chested hawk circled. On other visits there were caracaras dotting the paramo, stalking along on their longish legs. Even non-birders can enjoy this variety of birdlife, so many and so near. On rare occasions you may be fortunate enough to spot a spectacled bear, truly a once-in-a-lifetime occurrence!

Climbing and Accommodations

For the heartier, Cotopaxi is a climbing mecca. It can be climbed in a day, starting just after midnight. All climbers must be accompanied by a licensed guide. A number of professional climbing services are listed on the internet (see the appendix in this book for the climbing association), engaged by climbers from around the world.

For accommodation within the park there is the Tambopaxi hostel, which is largely used by climbers. It can be reached by car, and is comfortable if not luxurious. There is also the "Refugio" farther up the mountain, but the road is so rugged that climbers tend to hike up there from the

Tambopaxi level, and then stay for the few hours of night before they head to the top. For most visitors, however, who are in the park for the scenery and hiking the various trails along the paramo, the many hosterias and haciendas outside the park, including ones in Quito, offer a full range of accommodations.

BAÑOS

The drive to Baños from Cotopaxi takes about two and a half hours, with perhaps a stop along the way at a roadside cafe specializing in traditional Ecuadorean food. On this particular route there is a fascinating view of the lahars, a giant flow of mud, rocks, and ash that tore off from the Tungurahua volcano in 1989. From the viewpoint along the road, you can see a huge statue of a parrot sitting on a branch of a 12-meter-tall (40-foot) pole; on the other side is an empty branch that held a condor but was wiped out by the mud flow.

Traveling as fast as 190 kilometers (120 miles) an hour and 180 meters (600 feet) deep, lahars have destroyed whole cities around the world over the centuries. The lahar you see from the road was not that drastic, but nearby communities, such as Baños, were evacuated for some time as the volcano continued to rumble. In fact, Tungurahua continues to send out ash and smoke, and travel routes in the highlands often provide views of the activity. There is a national warning system and escape routes are signed, so the chances of your being at risk are minimal. There is a kind of thrill being so close in time and location to such a powerful geological phenomenon, however.

Baños is nestled in a narrow valley, alongside the Pastaza River. Tungurahua volcano dominates the scenery, which is spectacular. The valley sides are heavily forested, and there are sixty waterfalls in the immediate area. The town is small and easily walked from end to end. There is a beautiful church on the main plaza, the Church of the Virgin of the Holy Water.

Baños ("baths") is the hot springs center of Ecuador. There are a number of spas, of varying degrees of luxury, and a large public pool right in the center of town. It's a short walk from many of the accommodations in the town center. There are two pools, a small one in the scalding temperature range and a larger slightly cooler one that is crowded with folks of all ages and conditions.

This is also a hot spot for adventure sports—including hiking, river rafting, kayaking, canyoning, rock climbing, and mountain biking. There is a cable car across the Pastaza, as well as several zip lines. While you can plan ahead for these services, there are offices throughout the town where you can arrange something on the spot.

A Baños street in the rain

Baños is just a short distance away from the Amazonas zone of Ecuador, where you'll find excellent opportunities for varied birding trips. It is also possible to arrange with local companies or your own travel agent for anything from daylong to multiweek trips into the rain forest.

AVENUE OF THE WATERFALLS AND THE DEVIL'S CAULDRON

If your route takes you south toward Riobamba and then Cuenca, you'll be following the Avenue of the Waterfalls. The glacier-fed rivers originating in the Andes often make a series of precipitous plunges to the lowlands of Amazonas, to the east.

A side trip of just 16 kilometers (10 miles) will take you to one of the most famous falls in the country, Pailón del Diablo or the Devil's Cauldron. At a small reception building, you are offered a walking stick for your trek down the gorge of the Rio Verde to the ultimate destination of actually standing behind the falls! When I did this in 2010 the trail was rugged, and it was necessary to crawl on hands, knees, and stomach at one point, through a kind of slit cave in the canyon wall. Since then a stone trail has been extended, on either side of the river—there is a cable car to get across—so while you'll be glad for your walking stick for maneuvering the wet, concrete tiled path, you won't be terrifying your guide, as I did mine ("I thought you'd be the first client I was going to lose!"). It's not often that you can get so close to one of the many waterfalls you will be passing,

so do take the time for this experience, which is now much safer thanks to the completed trail.

Coming up from the waterfall we stopped at the cafe, which had an outdoor patio overlooking the dense vegetation lining the canyon walls. It turned out to be a birding highlight, with several species of tanagers, including the multicolored paradise tanager—flittering right in the plants leaning into the patio itself! I was too excited to get a clear picture, but the fuzzy one is fine, and the full beauty is still there in my mind's eye.

Another of the many waterfalls on this route is the Agoyan Waterfall, where there is a little cafe along the road, and a whole zip line set up. You might also wish to stop at the Manto de Novia (Bridal Veil Falls), where there is a cable car across the Pastaza River.

This route is also known as the Avenue of Orchids. The roadway is lined with towering granite walls on one side. Because there are hundreds of cracks and crevices where water seeps and trickles, you'll see hundreds of embedded orchids at certain times of the year. It was on this drive where I had one of those unplanned moments that make a trip memorable, a moment that is really only possible if you are in a vehicle that can stop when you want it to stop. Suddenly all along the edge of the road, from the ground and on up the stone walls, there were huge orchids! We came to a rapid halt, jumped out (being wary

The train tracks zigzag up the Devil's Nose.

of passing traffic), and got out the cameras. Our guide identified them as *Sobralia decora*. Between the birdlife and the plant life, anyone who loves beauty will never lack for exotic discoveries, at any and every turn.

DEVIL'S NOSE TRAIN RIDE

Farther south on the Pan-American Highway, the town of Alausi is where you can take the heart-stopping train ride along the Devil's Nose (Nariz del Diablo). The train descends nearly a kilometer in elevation over a ride of just 45 minutes each way. You leave from Alausi, stop for a visit in the small town of Silambe, and return the same way. The switchbacks are so severe, so numerous, that in the 1990s the tracks and train just slid down the steep slopes.

Since then the route, tracks, and train cars have been completely rebuilt or replaced. The train itself is designed for the visitor, with large windows and spacious, comfortable cars.

During your hour or so in Silambe, do visit the small ethnographic museum just up some stairs in the plaza. Also you are likely to be entertained by a folk dance troupe that performs in traditional dress on the plaza.

INGAPIRCA

Two hours' drive south of Alausi is Ingapirca, the ruins of a fortress and other structures built over centuries. Some segments were constructed by the Cañari people, who have lived in the area for some thousand years. Additional structures were built by the Inca during their brief occupation in the sixteenth century. During the occupation the Cañari were able to retain much of their way of life, including their monumental buildings, even though the Inca did add to these works. There are a number of these ruins in the highlands of Ecuador, but the largest and most intact is Ingapirca.

The ruins include terraces, food storage bins, housing, and most impressive, a conical structure assumed to be an Incan temple of the sun. The site is very well cared for, and visitors can walk freely within it. One of the many interesting features is the difference in the precision of stone masonry of the Inca and the earlier Cañari. The Incan stonework is characterized by straight lines and sharp,

clean edges, consisting of huge stones put together without mortar, similar to the construction of Machu Picchu. The Cañari stones tend to be smaller and less defined, with mortar having been used. As you walk along the pathways, it is easy to see these differences.

Ingapirca has great historical interest and is an important center for archaeological research. It is growing steadily as a tourism destination, and has a small museum as well as a gift shop. At an altitude of 3200 meters (10,500 feet), the weather changes rapidly. The car park is nearby, so you don't have to worry about exposure, but as in all of the highlands, wearing layered clothing and having a windbreaker jacket handy are always good

Ingapirca in the mist

ideas. There is an entrance fee to visit the site, with local guides.

Ingapirca and the area around it have a very different feel from the environment of the Avenue of the Volcanoes, which has a more moist atmosphere with its mix of heavily forested slopes and large swaths of grazing land. At Ingapirca the land is more open, more agricultural, with expansive fields of corn and other grains.

CUENCA—WORLD CULTURAL HERITAGE SITE

Cuenca was designated a UNESCO World Cultural Heritage Site in 1999. Founded in 1557, Cuenca is rich in history and very much a rapidly changing, dynamic city. It is Ecuador's third largest city, with a population of approximately three hundred thousand. There is a great deal of industrial development, yet it retains a sense of tradition. Cuenca is a very international city, becoming one of the most popular destinations for retirees from the United States and Europe.

Though Cuenca could occupy you for days or weeks, there are three essential places to visit, no matter the length of your stay: two historic churches, a monastery, and the home of the Panama hat. You will be at an altitude of 2500 meters (8200 feet), but focusing on the small central plaza and able to walk easily from place to place.

The two churches are located on either side of the main plaza, the Parque Calderón. One is the Church of the Shrine (Iglesia del Sagrario), informally known as the "Old Cathedral." The church was built by the Spanish colonizers for their exclusive use, with planning beginning in 1557 and actual construction starting ten years later. It was in regular use until the 1990s when the New Cathedral was completed. The Old Cathedral is a classic colonial basilica, with three naves branching off from a very high ceiling, replete with beautiful murals. There is a massive organ over the main entrance, and at the foot of the altar are life-sized sculptures of Christ and the disciples. The Old Church has been superseded by the New Church, and it now is the Museum for Religious Art and Restoration.

Right across the plaza is the New Cathedral (Catedral de la Inmaculada), which was one hundred years in the making, with construction ending in 1968. Its three marine-blue domes are stunning and reminiscent of the bulbous, onion-shaped domes of Russian Orthodox cathedrals. And as impressive as the domes and towers are, there is a sense of immediacy about this cathedral, because even if it is by no means small, it does not have the looming, almost daunting quality of the massive cathedrals of Quito, London, or Rome. The cathedral is built of a combination of local marbles and Carrera marbles from Italy. As you view the cathedral interior and exterior, the marble most on display is the highly polished Carrera.

There were plans to add a campanile to the cathedral, but in 1967 cracks had

The azure domes of the New Cathedral, Cuenca

begun to develop in the main structure, so further construction did not take place. You can see one of the cracks, located in the front of the building, above the main entrance. The stained glass windows are beautiful and especially interesting for their combination of Roman Catholic symbols and images and those reflecting the indigenous peoples' life and religious beliefs. This is an excellent example of "syncretism," this synthesis of elements of differing belief systems.

The cathedrals of Cuenca play a very large part in its identity as a World Cultural Heritage Site; but other very old buildings have been refurbished, and more recent ones are built in the original Spanish colonial style. It is an enriching experience just to stroll along peering at these buildings, sometimes going into a cafe or store that retains this style. One of the benefits of being a World Heritage Site is that funding can be provided to assist in protecting and renewing the precious built and natural environment, and this has played a role in the beauty and authenticity of Cuenca, especially its historic core.

Cuenca is divided by the Tomebamba River, which has the old town on one side and the new town on the other. The city has created walkways along the river, with fascinating views as you stroll there.

Monasterio de la Asunción

Another historic site, very much in use today, is the monastery of the Carmelite nuns, the Monasterio de la Asunción. The Carmelite order in Cuenca was founded in 1682. The monastery church was built in 1730, in the Baroque style.

The nuns are cloistered there, almost totally sequestered, completely draped in black robes, with their faces hidden behind veils. You will not be in any direct contact with them, but there is an indirect connection that is intriguing. For hundreds of years, there was sufficient support for the monastery and its inhabitants arising from the dowries of the young women who entered. As "brides of Christ" they traditionally would have brought a dowry. However, more recently, this income has not been sufficient to maintain the structure nor the women within. The Catholic Church provides some help as an institution, but the sisters themselves have created a way to generate some income by producing jams, herbal medicines, skin creams, and other items visitors may purchase. Because there can be no direct contact, visitors speak through a wooden mesh rotating "closet" with three vertical sections, asking for what they want. There is a pause while the item is collected from the storehouse area, then put on a shelf in another section of the closet, which is then rotated to the visitor's side where a small door can be opened and the item retrieved. All this is done with few words and no face-to-face contact.

The monastery is just a block away from Parque Calderón and is just across from the flower market and public market. The flower market is charming, and you will be awash with colors and scents. The public market has a huge variety of meats, fruits, and veggies, and garments of all kinds—some locally made, some from around the world (like the colorful array of running shoes).

Panama Hats

Cuenca is also famous for the so-called "Panama" hats, woven from the fibers of

Panama hats drying in the sun, Cuenca

the toquilla palm (not a true palm, but a palmlike plant). These hats have been made here in one form or another since the 1830s. The hat received international fame, and its name, when used by workers building the Panama Canal. Some hats are very high-fashion, and some are simple fedoras. They are very light, airy, and tough. While there are many qualities of Panama hats, and definitely some imitations, the highest-quality hats can be rolled up easily and still retain their shape when in use.

There are a number of producers in Cuenca and the vicinity, but the most famous one, Homero Ortega, hosts tours and has created the "Magic of the Hat" museum. The museum has photos of famous people around the world in their own Panamas. The tour is very interesting for seeing how the hats are woven and then blocked in pressing machines, and set out in the brilliant sun to dry.

CAJAS NATIONAL PARK

As you continue south toward Guayaquil, plan to spend at least a few hours walking in the last of the highland parks along your route, Cajas National Park. Its high point is 4167 meters (13,671 feet), though its lower elevation is about 3100 meters (10,000 feet). It is just 25 kilometers (15.5 miles) west of Cuenca, and is reached by a road that comes into the northern part of the park.

The drive into the park can be scary, because the road is very winding, with

chasms stretching out below in many places, and the road is often engulfed in clouds. This is because Cajas is on the western slopes of the Andes and thus captures the rising winds from the Pacific, with the air cooling as it rises, precipitating in the form of clouds, fog, and frequent rain. You will be relieved to reach one of the main destinations, the interpretive and tourism information center at the height of the park, at Toreadora lagoon. There is a cafe there as well.

The dominant landscape is open paramo, with its grassy, tundralike plant life that includes miniaturized flowers and a rich growth of fungi and mosses. However, in the many glacier-carved valleys and canyons you'll find forests up to the natural tree line, with diverse plants, including some endemic ones. The park is known for having the beautiful, and endangered *Fuchsia campi*, a tiny member of the willowherb family. It can be found at about 3300 meters (10,800 feet) elevation, and it is designated as protected because of its rarity.

Four major rivers arise from the glaciers in the park. Because the park is on the highest ridge of the Andes at this point, it forms the Continental Divide, with two of the rivers flowing to the east into the Amazonas area and the other two flowing west to the Pacific. The main road in the park crosses the Divide at the Three Crosses (Tres Cruces) viewpoint, where you can stop and walk up the hill to the very top and have magnificent views in all directions. But do look down at your feet also, for a close-up view of the paramo and its beautiful, tiny flowers.

Cajas National Park is an excellent place for walking, hiking, camping, and fishing. The wildlife is varied, with excellent birding. It is a good idea to arrange for a guide for any travel away from the short trails near the interpretive center, and especially if you intend to camp or fish. You can arrange for this through your tour company or through various services in Cuenca. A guide is a good idea, because you will want to have an informed person to tell you about this fascinating environment and to help you use your time well, and to be safe.

Bear in mind that you are at a high altitude and in a harsh environment. There can be sudden cloud cover right to the ground, very soft and often muddy terrain, lots of rain, and high winds. Stay hydrated and dress for variable weather. It will all be worth it.

I was not able to stay long in the park, but the view from Tres Cruces and my rather brief walk in the area have stayed fresh in my mind's eye and spirit ever since.

Continuing south, you will be passing through more open landscapes, with farms and wide pastures, as the altitude lessens and the land slopes toward the sea. It becomes a whole different world. Guayaquil, the endpoint of the journey from the highlands to the lowlands of Ecuador, is covered in chapter 22 as part of the coastal zone.

21

THE RAIN FOREST OF ECUADOR

The rain forest is east of the Andes, as the slope descends to sea level. The moisture that arises from the cycle of respiration of the trees below, becoming the frequent torrential rains, give this ecological zone its name.

I have spent time in the rain forest of Ecuador on each of my trips. My first visit, some thirty-five years ago, was the most "basic." I signed on in Canada for a canoe tour to the Cuyubeno area, very near the border with Peru. This was before Cuyubeno was a national reserve or park. I went with my two teenaged nephews, landing in Lago Agrio, and baking in the sun in a large, unshaded cargo "canoe" for ten hours down the Agua Rico River, a "yellow" river, with its source in the Andes. The canoe was about 18 meters (60 feet) long and 1.8 meters (6 feet) wide, and it often went aground, requiring us to get out and help push the boat off sandbars. We got used to jumping over the side into waist-deep water to

help free the canoe, hopping back in, and carrying on. Then it was another hour or so in a small dugout canoe, holding eight of us, wending our way along a narrow "black river," its source being runoff from the rains in the forest.

Finally, the forest opened up and we arrived at a lake, where we camped near its shore, sleeping in an abandoned, palm-roofed communal house, used by the indigenous peoples now and then as they followed the game that was a major part of their diet. We took walks along trails that couldn't be seen, since it was the wet season and they were covered in a half meter of water. We heard the cooing sounds of the tinamou at night and the metallic shriek of the screaming piha bird in the daytime. We would borrow a small dugout and use the diamond-shaped paddles to cruise quietly on the lake, with dragonflies zipping around us, orchids dripping from the trees standing in the water. We took pictures of the tiny snout-nosed bats

Embarking on the Napo River to an eco-lodge in the rain forest

dozing on the underside of slanting dead tree snags poking out of the lake.

As for food, on that particular trip, it was globs of dough fried in fat, or a chopped-up piranha floating in barely boiled water. We had a wonderful time, but there were some real risks along the way. It was a lesson in making sure that a tour company is reputable, and that it has firm connections with its Ecuador partners, who will be the ones actually providing your services in the rain forest. (We got a refund.)

But that particular adventure, now quite long ago, was when rain-forest tourism was poorly organized. It is a whole different world now, and while the now grown-up nephews and I still regale ourselves with stories about the food and the sunstroke and the uninformed guide flown in from Quito at the last minute, your visit will also be an adventure, but in the best sense. Every one of my subsequent trips to the rain forest have been very well done—the trip in, the time spent there, the travel out.

STAYING IN AN ECO-LODGE

Your visit to the rain forest will be professionally managed, with guided walks and evening paddles, and great food. You'll also have time on your own, to have an intensive experience of the rain forest. Of course, it would take a lifetime to be truly familiar with this rich and increasingly endangered environment, but even the standard visit of four or five days in an eco-lodge will stay in your heart forever.

Your rain-forest visit should be arranged by an eco-tourism company—there is essentially no other way to access the rain forest for a visit of a few days. You will fly either to Coca or Lago Agrio, be met by staff from your lodge, and then take perhaps an hour's ride in a large, covered but open-air cargo or transport boat. Then at a shoreline dock you'll transfer to a smaller canoe for your group, and will wend your way on a black river to a lovely lake with a marvelous lodge on a hillside.

There are a number of eco-lodges located in readily accessible (by air) national parks, reserves, and privately owned nature reserves throughout the Amazonas area of Ecuador. Several of the lodges are owned and managed by the local indigenous tribes. This is part of their efforts to sustain their traditional way of life, by ensuring that its value is recognized and protected, and to participate in the economic benefits that can come with truly responsible eco-tourism.

But regardless of who owns the lodge and grounds, indigenous peoples are now always paired with the lodge-based guides for all of the hikes, bird-watching, canoeing, fishing, and other wildlife watching that you will do. The lodge-based guides tend to be fully trained and licensed, and are fluent in Spanish and English, and with a number having other languages as well. The indigenous guides speak Quechua, or a version of it, and have a working knowledge of Spanish. The lodge-based guides are increasingly

familiar with Quechua. So between the two of them you will find that you can easily understand the explanations about what you are seeing or hearing, smelling, or (possibly) touching as you walk along the trails or canoe in the lake.

The lodges will vary in the degree of luxury and costs, but I have stayed in five different ones, over nine of my ten trips to date, and several times in two different ones of them—an indigenous one and a private one—and have found all of them to be comfortable, with large, airy cabins, clean bathrooms with showers, good beds, excellent food, and good guides. I've been led by several of the guides for more than one trip, because they "migrate" from lodge to lodge over the years, and some also guide in Quito or in the highlands haciendas. They know their birds, the plants, the history, and they work well with their indigenous counterparts.

Potential visitors sometimes wonder if they will be comfortable in the rainforest environment. They wonder about the heat, bugs, the energy required. There is no doubt it is very hot and, above all, humid. You will be constantly damp, even if you don't think you are sweating. It is essential to drink copious amounts of fluids. The supply of fruit juices seems to be limitless, and all lodges have treated water and a bar in their main lodge building. (You pay for soft drinks and liquor; drinks are not included in your accommodation costs.) Do carry a water bottle with you.

There are mosquitoes (see chapter 16), so bring a good bug repellent. The screening of the cabins and the mosquito netting that is lowered each evening over all beds, as you are having dinner elsewhere, seem to minimize discomfort and bites where you are living day to day. But on the trails or walking around the lodge grounds, repellent is useful.

Sunscreen is very important, though much of your time is spent in the shade of the dense forest.

Do refer back to chapter 17 about cloud forest eco-lodges on the western slope of the Andes; they are equally rich, dense, diverse. Visit both environments if

you have a chance. Also, see chapter 16 for more details on clothing.

SEEING AND HEARING IN THE RAIN FOREST

The tours offer a regular program of activities, led by trained guides. Each of the eco-lodges has a special viewing platform that brings you over the dense canopy of the rain forest. One lodge has a tower surrounding a giant, buttressed kapok tree, with space for fifteen people or more to stand, sit, walk around a bit, use spotting scopes the guide brings along, take pictures, and absorb the ambience. Another lodge has a 275-meter (900-foot) catwalk

Squirrel monkey on a dock along the Napo River

from tower to tower, an adventure in itself. On the ground you will have walks part of each day, guided canoe rides for some time, perhaps go for a swim, or fish for the toothy piranhas of fame. (They swim in the deeper water, you swim nearer the surface—it all works out; just don't have any open wounds to attract them.) There are always evening canoe rides, where the guide has a spotlight and you can see the alligatorlike caiman along the edges of the lake, or get a glimpse of a capybara coming down to drink. Everyone is quiet, causing as little disturbance as possible.

One of the most memorable canoe rides for me was just before dusk, as we paddled along the lake's edge. Suddenly we were just a few meters from a troop of squirrel monkeys that were feeding in the trees beside us. They go out to the edge of a branch for some fruit, and just as the branch dips close to the water, nearly swamping the monkey, it leaps up to the next branch, runs along it, takes a bit of something, dips down again and bounces back up—over and over. Seeing such a sight is wonderful in itself, but is also a reminder that the rapid destruction of the rain forest, even within some park and reserve areas, threatens these precious animals—as it does the whole ecosystem.

Another reminder comes from howler monkeys, not often seen, but often heard in the night. They sound like some kind of distant whooshing sound, unearthly, ethereal, strange. At first you can't be sure you are hearing anything—it is so subtle

and so unlike anything you've heard elsewhere, so there is nothing to compare it with. They are supposed to be one of the loudest animals in the world, but somehow the sound is not so much loud as it is just weird. But your guide will tell you that's what you're hearing, maybe as you are sitting in the main lodge of an evening, after your dinner and your canoe ride. Once your ear is tuned to it, the howlers will be an integral part of your rain-forest experience.

Rain-Forest Birding

Then there are the birds. With some fifteen hundred species of birds, it's rather frustrating that they are not easy to see in the rain forest. Intact rain forest is at two levels—ground and hundreds of feet up in the canopy. The ground cover tends to be very dense, and birds there are hard to see. Way up in the towers you are above the canopy, but the birds are mostly right within the foliage below, and equally hard to spot, though you will be delighted with the occasional flight of screaming parrots passing at your level. However, birding can be excellent where there are open spaces along banks of rivers or lakes, or near gardens of the communities of the indigenous peoples, or at the edges of the compound of the eco-lodge.

This is not to suggest that you won't be seeing a large number of species new to you, you will be. But it does point out the importance of having birding guides. The eco-lodge may have guides who are

Two parrot species at a clay lick along the Napo River

expert birders, but whether or not they do, the lodge can also engage an indigenous birding expert to go with you and the staff guide, to help with translation. With the indigenous guide's knowledge, their lifetime of observing every animal and plant in the area, they see what you could never see on your own. They hear what you would never hear, or you might hear something but would not even know that it was a bird you were hearing, much less know which kind it was. I remember one indigenous guide in particular. We would be walking along, quietly, and he would stop, point to a place on a branch 200 feet above us, and say the name to the lodge guide. If we were fast, we could pick out the bird, perhaps no bigger than

a chickadee, with our binoculars. "The red-capped manakin." And so it went.

Other Beauties

The same is true for insects—a leaf turned over by the indigenous guide so that you can see a bizarre stick bug, a colorful beetle, a tiny frog. You probably would never have seen it otherwise. The butterflies are exquisite: the huge turquoise morphos slowly flapping along an open path, the clearwings sipping from a mud puddle by the walkway, the heliconians sunning on a leaf not far from your head. Then there are the mushrooms, the fungi, the orchids, the bromeliads lining the branches of trees. The rain forest is endless in its beauty.

22

COASTAL ECUADOR

T he Ecuadorean coast is essentially a narrow plain bordered by rising slopes of the western Andes. The coast stretches from Esmeraldas in the north, near the border with Columbia, to just beyond Salinas at the southern end. The road distance is about 500 kilometers (310 miles). I have not had a chance to visit this area very often, but can highlight some particular areas suggested by guides I have known for years. I hope to get to many of these places on my next visit. This chapter covers southern to mid-coastal Ecuador.

Ecuador's tourism policy is focused on creating its own distinctive approach to development of residences or tourism services along the coast. It is not to be another Mexican beach resort strip, but rather a series of communities, parks, and reserves that sustain the environment and reflect local cultures and ways of life. For example, in most places homes or accommodations cannot be built directly on the beaches, but must blend unobtrusively into the fields and woodlands beyond the sable sand and dunes. In the larger communities this has not always been achieved, but the goal is in place.

There are two main ways to start your visit to the coast. Most visitors begin their coastal trip by driving north for about three hours from Guayaquil, coming into Salinas at the south end of the coast. It is also possible to drive for seven hours from Quito to Manta in the central coast. There are buses as well that take either of these routes. However, the modern city of Manta has an airport for flights within Ecuador, and flying there and then renting a car and driving the coast with your tour or on your own is a good way to visit this fascinating and varied environment. The highway is called the Sun Road (La Ruta del Sol).

Give yourself at least three days and nights for the trip, whichever direction you decide to go. The descriptions below will take you first to Guayaquil and nearby communities and parks. Then there is a leap to Manta, with highlights of places to visit as you drive south.

GUAYAQUIL AND ENVIRONS

Guayaquil is the largest city in Ecuador, and its main port. The city was founded by the Spanish in 1538, though there was habitation millennia before that. At the present it has a population of some 3.75 million. With Guayaquil becoming the primary arrivals-and-departures destination for travelers to the Galapagos, the city is working on developing its attractions for visitors, and on changing its reputation as a rather rough-hewn port city. It has a number of very appealing places, so it is worth your while to set aside several days for a visit.

First of all, this is an equatorial coastal environment, very hot and moist. The land around the city is largely agricultural, including huge pasturelands for cattle and hectare upon hectare devoted to rice and fruit cultivation. Until recently, the main crop in the area was the cacao bean, for chocolate.

Fortunes were made by the few families who owned the vast majority of the land, and those involved in shipping also did very well. Huge mansions were built, with the development of all kinds of cultural and entertainment activities and buildings. But this has changed over time, and while there is still considerable wealth, it is not on display in the center of town as it once was.

The town itself has been razed by fire repeatedly over the centuries. It was a wooden city, not built of stone as in the cities of the highlands. The most recent fire was in the 1920s.

As part of its development efforts, the city has created the Parque Historico (Historic Park). Those few buildings that survived that latest fire were preserved and now have been restored, and others in the same style have been added into the Parque area. There are residences, stores, and a hospital. This is all in the Samborondón district of the city, just across the Guayas River, about a 20-minute taxi ride from the downtown area. The Parque also has a botanical garden and a zoo.

A striking example of urban renewal is the 3-kilometer-long (1.9-mile) Malecón 2000, a wide, colorful river-walk along the Guayas River. It is lined with shops, cafes, decorative fountains, benches, and shaded areas. Cultural events and other entertainments often happen there, and it is a wonderful place to absorb local flavor and be out in a cooling breeze. Welcoming to all, the Malecón is well-patrolled and you will be comfortable and at ease there. It closes at eight in the evening, just as darkness comes here at the equator.

Also not to be missed are the iguanas of Guayaquil. These land iguanas are very different from the ones you will have seen in the Galapagos. They are more slender, with long legs and a fast, springy gait.

Most are bright green, though some are more olive colored. They can grow up to a good meter in length. The greatest concentration of them is found in the Seminario Park, in the center of the city. They are wonderful to watch, whether dashing across the grass, basking in the sun, or draped over the branches of trees above.

CERRO BLANCO RESERVE

A 20-minute drive away from Guayaquil is a wonderful opportunity for birders—and remember, this is a whole different habitat than those you have visited elsewhere in our travels. This is a "dry tropical forest," of which there are very few left in the world, though there are also mangrove swamp ecosystems. This destination is the Cerro Blanco Reserve. You can go by yourself and walk the nearby trails, but to go farther into the mix of forest and mangrove swamps you will want to go with one of the bilingual guides, who charge a very modest rate for the day. The reserve is also home to many mammals, including various monkey species. There is a modest campground, a cabin that can be rented, and a cafe. More than two hundred species of birds have been recorded there, so take at least a day trip there, whether with your own tour group, or on your own.

MONTAÑITA

At the southern end of the Ecuadorean coast is the village of Montañita. It is 170 kilometers (105 miles) almost directly west of Guayaquil, somewhat over a two-and-a-half-hour drive. In contrast to the rather low-key approach to tourism of coastal communities farther north, Montañita is known as the surfing and party hub of the coast. The surfing is world-class, the cafes and bars are ubiquitous, and music and good times are on a 24-hour schedule. There are many hostels for the surfing crowd, and a few hotels. You'll find some accommodations a few minutes away from the populous downtown section, usually on quiet beaches. They are within walking distance of the action, but provide a getaway for those who want it.

MANTA

Visitors planning to travel the La Ruta del Sol will drive south from the city of Manta. A deep-water port, Manta traditionally has been a major center for tuna fishing, both industrial and sport. However, tuna are being overfished around the world, and even though there are some brief periods each year when tuna fishing is banned, the trends in species depletion continue. On the more upbeat side, Manta is very popular for the variety of water sports practiced there—board surfing, kite-board surfing, and body-boarding. International competitions are held here for these activities. There is a 1.6-kilometer (1-mile) Malecón (boardwalk) along the waterfront, lined with restaurants, shops, and bars, but I suggest that you visit in the daytime only. Manta is also a stopover for cruise ships, which frequent the coastline from October through March.

Manta's cultural center, the Museo Centro Cultural Manta, is just across the street from the Malecón. It features artifacts from the Valdivian peoples, who lived in the area from 3500 to 1500 BC.

REFUGIO DE VIDA SILVESTRE, MARINO Y COSTERO PACOCHE

Just 25.5 kilometers (16 miles) south of Manta is a whole different world—the 13,040-hectare (32,220-acre) Refugio de Vida Silvestre, Marino y Costero Pacoche. This is a national reserve for protecting the forest, wildlife, and coastal marine life of the area. The forest is one of the very few remaining tropical dry forests. Also known as "drought-deciduousness," in the dry season many of the species of tree respond by dropping their leaves, but this is not the same seasonal process of the deciduous forests of northern North America (maples, oaks). There are hiking trails, a little cafe, and two cabins for overnight stays. The birdlife is rich, with some 150 species recorded there, though in a fairly dense forest, your own sightings may be relatively modest in number. There are some 350 species of plants, many characteristic of the dry forest. With luck, you'll hear and even see the resident howler monkeys.

MACHALILLA NATIONAL PARK

As you continue south, about two hours' drive from Manta is the Machalilla National Park, in the province of Manabi. The park encompasses 55,000 hectares (about 212 square miles) of mixed dry forest, low cloud forest, and both sandy and rocky shorelines. Because of its diverse habitat, ranging from sea level to fingers of the lower slopes of the Andes meeting the seashore in places, there are 270 species of birds recorded in the park. Some are very rare and their survival is severely threatened.

There are a number of islets along the coast of the park, some of which can be visited. Others are off-limits to land visits, but excellent places for snorkeling from a boat. Small villages along the Ruta del Sol include Salango, which has a museum exhibiting artifacts from pre-Columbian cultures that lived in the area for millennia. Very diverse, they include the Valdivia, Machalilla–Engoroy Chorrera, Bahia, Guangala, and Manta cultures.

PUERTO LOPEZ

The village of Puerto Lopez and its surrounding area are a hub of tourism activities. This also is the whale-watching center of the coast from June to September. Some two to three thousand humpback whales visit this area for their mating and calving season. Tour companies provide half- or all-day excursions out to see these giants of the sea, and some offer activities such as hiking, bicycling, birding, and boat trips for snorkeling to islets and also to the Isla de la Plata.

Whale diving near Manta (Juan Silva)

ISLA DE LA PLATA

The Isla de la Plata is a part of the Machalilla National Park. It is sometimes called the "little Galapagos" of Ecuador, because of its dry, rocky terrain and shoreline and its similar birdlife—especially the nesting blue-footed boobies (but no Darwin's finches). It is a protected area, reached by an hour-and-a-half boat ride from Puerto Lopez, done as a day trip. Most boat tours provide a light packed lunch and offer snorkeling equipment rentals; you can make arrangements with tour companies in the town.

Once on the Isla, you'll find guides available to tell you about this very special place and to accompany you along the various trails, which range from about 1.6 kilometers (1 mile) to 6 kilometers (4 miles). Bring water, sunscreen, a hat, and a windbreaker, and you'll be fine. You may want to snorkel toward the end of your day. The rocky shoreline is an excellent place to cool off and enjoy the underwater world.

For accommodations in the park itself and surrounding areas along this part of the coast, there are a few eco-lodges and some modest hotels or hostels. If you are with a tour, the company will take care of this and if you are on your own, the internet should be helpful.

This ends your travel along the La Ruta del Sol. Whichever direction you take, wherever you go, there is something for everyone along the way.

Path to Devil's Cauldron, Ecuador

APPENDIX

RESOURCES

Travel Information
- International Galapagos Tour Operators Association (IGTOA), www.igtoa.org
- Ecuadorean Mountain Guide Association (ESGUIM, office in Quito with international partnerships), www.aseguim.nicotinamedia.com/ingles/contacto_escuela.html

Key Organizations
The following organizations support conservation and community-building in the Galapagos:
- Galapagos Conservancy, www.galapagos.org
- Charles Darwin Foundation, www.darwinfoundation.org
- Galapagos National Park Directorate, www.galapagospark.org

IUCN RED LIST CONSERVATION STATUS CRITERIA
The International Union for Conservation of Nature (IUCN) lists the following criteria for conservation status on its website, http://jr.iucnredlist.org/documents/RedListGuidelines.pdf. Species are classified into nine groups, set through criteria, such as rate of decline, population size, area of geographic distribution, and degree of population and distribution fragmentation. When discussing the IUCN Red List, the official term *threatened* is a grouping of three categories: critically endangered, endangered, and vulnerable.

- **Extinct (EX)**—No known individuals remaining.
- **Extinct in the wild (EW)**—Known only to survive in captivity or as a naturalized population outside its historic range.
- **Critically endangered (CR)**—Extremely high risk of extinction in the wild.
- **Endangered (EN)**—High risk of extinction in the wild.
- **Vulnerable (VU)**—High risk of endangerment in the wild.
- **Near threatened (NT)**—Likely to become endangered in the near future.
- **Least concern (LC)**—Lowest risk. Does not qualify for a more at risk category. Widespread and abundant taxa are included in this category.
- **Data deficient (DD)**—Not enough data to make an assessment of its risk of extinction.
- **Not evaluated (NE)**—Has not yet been evaluated against the criteria.

INDEX

TRAVEL NOTES

TRAVEL NOTES

WILDLIFE LIST

WILDLIFE LIST

ABOUT THE AUTHOR

Gwyneth Bowen

Marylee Stephenson's early interest in birding quickly evolved into a determination to visit the Galapagos Islands. It was years before this dream became reality, but she has visited the islands ten times over the past thirty-five years in watercraft ranging from a simple, hand-hewn fishing boat with no electricity, modest plumbing, and a speed of 5 knots, to the most swift and luxurious cruise ship. She has traveled with children, seniors, experts, and visitors who weren't even sure why they were there but were all glad they'd come. In preparing each edition of this guidebook, Marylee has supplemented her own Galapagos' experiences and research through numerous interviews with scientists, conservation groups, guides, visitors, crews, and captains. A dedicated naturalist, Marylee is widely published and has written a number of related articles, made presentations, and taught courses about the Galapagos Islands and how to prepare for and enjoy travel there. She has a doctorate in sociology and is a professional storyteller and occasional stand-up comic. She lives in Vancouver, British Columbia.

MOUNTAINEERS BOOKS

SKIPSTONE   BRAIDED RIVER

recreation • lifestyle • conservation

MOUNTAINEERS BOOKS is a leading publisher of mountaineering literature and guides—including our flagship title, *Mountaineering: The Freedom of the Hills*—as well as adventure narratives, natural history, and general outdoor recreation. Through our two imprints, Skipstone and Braided River, we also publish titles on sustainability and conservation. We are committed to supporting the environmental and educational goals of our organization by providing expert information on human-powered adventure, sustainable practices at home and on the trail, and preservation of wilderness.

The Mountaineers, founded in 1906, is a 501(c)(3) nonprofit outdoor activity and conservation organization whose mission is "to explore, study, preserve, and enjoy the natural beauty of the outdoors." One of the largest such organizations in the United States, it sponsors classes and year-round outdoor activities throughout the Pacific Northwest, including climbing, hiking, backcountry skiing, snowshoeing, bicycling, camping, paddling, and more. The Mountaineers also supports its mission through its publishing division, Mountaineers Books, and promotes environmental education and citizen engagement. For more information, visit The Mountaineers Program Center, 7700 Sand Point Way NE, Seattle, WA 98115-3996; phone 206-521-6001; www.mountaineers.org; or email info@mountaineers.org.

Our publications are made possible through the generosity of donors and through sales of more than 600 titles on outdoor recreation, sustainable lifestyle, and conservation. To donate, purchase books, or learn more, visit us online:

MOUNTAINEERS BOOKS
1001 SW Klickitat Way, Suite 201 • Seattle, WA 98134
800-553-4453 • mbooks@mountaineersbooks.org • www.mountaineersbooks.org

Mountaineers Books is proud to be a corporate sponsor of The Leave No Trace Center for Outdoor Ethics, whose mission is to promote and inspire responsible outdoor recreation through education, research, and partnerships • The Leave No Trace program is focused specifically on human-powered (nonmotorized) recreation • Leave No Trace strives to educate visitors about the nature of their recreational impacts and offers techniques to prevent and minimize such impacts • Leave No Trace is best understood as an educational and ethical program, not as a set of rules and regulations • For more information, visit www.lnt.org, or call 800-332-4100.

OTHER TITLES YOU MIGHT ENJOY FROM MOUNTAINEERS BOOKS

Trekking in Ecuador
Robert and Daisy Kunstaetter
The definitive travel guide to exploring the
unique diversity and splendor in Ecuador

Ecuador: A Climbing Guide
Yossi Brain
A straightforward, well-illustrated guide to
twenty of the country's major peaks,
including the volcanic Big 10

The Art of Rough Travel: From the Peculiar to the Practical, Advice from a 19th-Century Explorer
Sir Francis Galton
Edited by Katharine Harmon
Recounts Galton's adventures as one of the first Europeans
to explore the interior of southwestern Africa

Steller's Island: Adventures of a Pioneer Naturalist in Alaska
Dean Littlepage
The fascinating tale of the first
scientist to set foot in the
western half of North America

Travels to the Edge: A Photo Odyssey
Art Wolfe
Adventurous and stunning images depicting
the landscapes, wildlife, and cultures of Alaska,
Bolivia, Madagascar, Patagonia, Peru, the
US Southwest, and beyond